05/13                                                    DEA

Books should be returned or renewed by the last date
above. Renew by phone **08458 247 200** or online
*www.kent.gov.uk/libs*    03000 41 31 31

364 · 152309   WITHDRAW

**Libraries & Archives**     CUSTOMER SERVICE EXCELLENCE   UK   The Government Standard

Kent County Council

This is a unique book, eloquent, moving and challenging to
everyone who reads it. Margaret speaks from her heart: a
heart of profound                              t of deep
love and terrible                              y her
luminous faith. T

**Archbis**

D1464733

C333320322

The words "remarkable" and "extraordinary" have been over used and lost their meaning. But these adjectives are the only way to describe a remarkable story which turns ordinary folk into extraordinary characters. Few tales have life-changing consequences. But this one did. I like to think of myself as a hardened hack, measured and someone who doesn't give way to hyperbole. I read *Jimmy, A Legacy of Peace* and started to cry for a young man I never knew, who was at the wrong place at the wrong time and yet would unwittingly sacrifice his life to make us better.

This is a story of our times, so hauntingly captured by Justin Butcher. It provides a searingly intimate portrayal of an ordinary family picked by fate to be a twenty-first century symbol of hope. It tells of real, honest, decent people who never wanted any of this. It is a warts and all, unsugary journey into a family's hell and how they get out the other end, scathed, scarred yet their love growing even stronger.

I'm grateful I met Margaret and Barry. Our paths would probably not have crossed but for this tragic tale. Their work for CAFOD and their Foundation and this book are testament to human endeavour, human triumph in the face of an unfortunately human evil. It shows us that kindness to one another is a much, much better use of our emotion than cruelty. Barry and Margaret say: "Everything we do is about hope, joy and peace." And that comes across every page of Jimmy's story. Their account makes me know for certain that I'm lucky to have a wife and daughter to love.

Every year I lecture a group of first year journalism students at the University of Lincoln. Every year I tell them about Jimmy Mizen and how an incredible couple made me a better journalist. But if I could turn back time and make wishes come true, then I'd ask that this ordinary husband and wife could get their son back. Every one of us should be made to read *Jimmy, A Legacy of Peace*. We'll be the better for it.

**Barnie Choudhury**

# Jimmy

## A Legacy of Peace

*by Margaret Mizen*
*with Justin Butcher*

· · · · · · · · · · · ·

dedicated to the memory and enduring legacy of

**Jimmy Mizen**

(9 May 1992 – 10 May 2008)

Text copyright © 2013 Margaret Mizen and Justin Butcher

This edition copyright © 2013 Lion Hudson

The right of Margaret Mizen and Justin Butcher to be identified
as the authors of this work has been asserted by them in accordance
with the Copyright, Designs and Patents Act 1988.

All rights reserved. No part of this publication may be reproduced
or transmitted in any form or by any means, electronic or mechanical,
including photocopy, recording, or any information storage and
retrieval system, without permission in writing from the publisher.

Published by Lion Books
an imprint of
**Lion Hudson plc**
Wilkinson House, Jordan Hill Road,
Oxford OX2 8DR, England
www.lionhudson.com/lion

ISBN 978 0 7459 5579 7
e-ISBN 978 0 7459 5886 6

First edition 2013

**Acknowledgments**
p. 9: Extract from "Thought for the Day" by Sister Una McCreesh
on BBC Radio 4. Reprinted by permission of the BBC.
p. 86: Extract from "On Eagle's Wings" copyright © 1979, Jan
Michael Joncas. Published by OCP. 5536 NE Hassalo, Portland,
OR 97213. All rights reserved. Used with permission.
p. 87: Extracts from *Life of the Beloved* by Henri Nouwen copyright © Henri
Nouwen, 2002. Reprinted by permission of The Crossroad Publishing
Company.
p. 88: Warmest thanks to Coldplay, for kind permission to quote lyrics
from "Fix You".
p. 92: Warmest thanks to the estate of Bob Marley, for kind permission to
quote lyrics from "Three Little Birds".
pp. 130–31: Extract from "No Hiding Place" by Erwin James in
*The Guardian*, 23 May 2008 copyright © Erwin James, 2008. Reprinted
by permission of *The Guardian* and Erwin James.
p. 163: Warmest thanks to Rolf Løvland and Brendan Graham, for kind
permission to quote lyrics from "You Raise Me Up".
pp. 202–203: Extract from "The party leader who dares will win the
battle over politics of the soul" by Mary Riddell in the *Telegraph*, 19
December 2011 copyright © Mary Riddell, 2011. Reprinted by
permission of the *Telegraph*.
p. 204: Extract from article on *The Independent* website by Stefano
Hatfield copyright © Stefano Hatfield, 2012. Reprinted by permission
of *The Independent*.

A catalogue record for this book is available from the British Library

Printed and bound in the UK, March 2013, LH26

# Contents

# Author's Note

It's been my privilege and pleasure to work closely with Margaret Mizen and her family on this book over the past three years. Wherever possible, the story is told in her own words, from Margaret's perspective; these episodes are set in an italic font throughout. Elsewhere, I have recreated episodes from Jimmy's life and death, based on interviews and conversations with family members and friends, the testimony of witnesses and other commentators, newspaper articles, and television reportage, and these passages are set in plain text throughout. I met Margaret and her family for the first time in the summer of 2010 (see Chapter 12) and from that point onwards I become a character in their story, as a friend and collaborator, and so the narrative acknowledges my presence.

I would like to thank the many people and organizations whose encouragement and support have contributed invaluably to the writing of this book: Tom O'Connor, Monica Conmee, Juliana Barrett and Linda Jones and all at the Catholic Agency for Overseas Development (CAFOD), who supported the book's early development and of course organized the remarkable visit to Kenya in September 2011; Ali Hull and all at Lion Hudson whose belief in the book has been sustained with astonishing patience over many changes of tack; the Reverend Dave Tomlinson and all of my community at St Luke's, West Holloway; the Reverend Professor Richard Burridge, in whose house many of the interviews and much of the writing took place, for much friendship and advice; my friends Harvey Brough, Andrew Harrison, Rupert Mason, and Dan Northam-Jones, for their interest and great encouragement throughout; my literary agents Charles Walker and Katy Jones, for their assistance, interest, and support and, of course, my wife Nancy and my family, in particular my eldest son Benedict and my mother Rosemary, who have followed every twist and turn of the journey with unfailing confidence in me, and great encouragement.

Last and most of all I would like to thank Margaret and Barry Mizen and their family. A great friendship has grown between us over these three years, which I treasure, but more than this, I feel I have grown to know Jimmy over this time, even to share in mourning his loss and celebrating his life. I would like to thank Jimmy and his family for allowing me to be a part of their story.

Justin Butcher
New Year's Day, 2013
London

Believe me, Mama, there is no injustice willingly accepted that does not bear fruit a hundredfold, and receive its just reward, prodigal beyond our comprehension. Do not think that all the sorrows that have overwhelmed our family in recent years are useless... the law of life is that some pay for others: young branches full of sap are cut back and old, unproductive boughs left in their place. This seems unjust, and it would be, if a compensation far outweighing anything life could offer were not given to these victims, who are by the very fact privileged... It is only recently that I have come to understand the meaning of the cross. It is at once prodigious and atrocious: prodigious because it gives us life, and atrocious because if we do not accept to be crucified, all life is denied us. This is a great mystery, and blessed are the persecuted.

**Jacques Fesch**

*Jacques Fesch was a murderer executed in Paris in 1957, who experienced a profound conversion in the last year of his life and wrote such visionary letters of spiritual devotion from prison that he was proposed for beatification by the Roman Catholic Church.*

A few weeks ago, I found myself in a school hall with a hundred fifteen-year-olds from ten schools across our diocese. With them, I sat spellbound as Barry and Margaret Mizen recounted the day on which their son Jimmy was killed in a senseless act of violence. The story was as vividly present to those parents as on the day he died and as it will remain every day of their lives. But what those students and I took away was not the story of shock and horror, which it certainly was, but a positive sense of hope and confidence in the power of ordinary people, through their faith, to turn the bad to good. The Mizen family story is well known: they made national headlines by immediately seeking forgiveness not revenge. That simple, but far from easy, step today finds them as peace leaders at home and abroad. We all went away from that conference fired with enthusiasm, each a little more conscious of the good within us, the power of God and our ability to change life around us.

… We each of us inescapably shape our world. If we cramp ourselves in fear, apathy and despair grow. If we let the good within us surface, hope and happiness can blossom.

**Sister Una McCreesh, *Thought for the Day*, BBC Radio 4, 28 December 2012**

# 1

## Saturday Morning

10 May 2008

On any other Saturday, Jimmy would have been at work. He'd have rolled out of bed, bleary-eyed after a night out with his friends, and ambled sleepily downstairs to rummage for some breakfast amidst the good-natured chaos of the busy family kitchen, where his parents and his six brothers, two sisters and a nephew, not to mention girlfriends, boyfriends, family friends, and schoolmates came and went in a continuous thoroughfare and the fridge door never seemed to stay shut for more than a minute. He'd have greeted his mum, Margaret, with that incorrigible smile, dark eyes blinking through tousled teenager hair, and joshed or wrestled with one or other of his brothers, or maybe exchanged a hug with his devoted older sister Sammy T.

If he'd been up in time, he'd have had a lift to work in his dad's van, father and son trundling off to the shoe-mender's shop in Sidcup. Barry and his Saturday-boy Jimmy trading well-worn family jokes and whistling the "Sailor's Hornpipe" together, slow and deadpan at first, then quicker and quicker, accelerating at each reprise, chuckling and snorting, faster and sillier, till they both succumbed to helpless giggling.

Given a tenner as usual at lunchtime, Jimmy would have asked, "What d'you want, Dad?" and got the customary response – "Surprise me." As always, he'd have returned a few minutes later with a cheese roll for his dad, an armful of food for himself, and no change. And that winning smile.

This was how it would have been on any other Saturday.

But Jimmy had turned sixteen yesterday, so he'd been awarded a day off work. Monday would be his last day at school before GCSEs, and then he'd be leaving to start his apprenticeship at Leathermarket JMB in the autumn. Today felt like one of those special days, an in-between day, a threshold, maybe, between the end of childhood and the beginning of something else, the first day of being sixteen. So Jimmy was off work and up early that Saturday. He was excited, feeling on the brink of change and new possibilities. You could leave home if you were sixteen, or get married; you could join the army, ride a moped, drink in a pub, fly a glider, order your own passport... all the rules changed at sixteen.

In the summer, his two best pals from school were heading off to California; one of them had an uncle who worked at Disneyland. Jimmy was desperate to go with them, and last night his mum and dad had bowled him over with their birthday gift: some new shirts, a pair of sunglasses, and a card, with the words inside, "IOU £500." His ticket to California! Jimmy hugged his parents ecstatically, a warm three-way hug, a precious birthday moment. Towering over his mum, and half a head taller than his dad at six foot four, Jimmy looked very fine in his new shirt, smart white with a thin brown stripe, a gentle, handsome giant with a sparkling smile, and they'd told him how proud of him they were, how much they loved him.

"I love you, Mum," he'd said, "I love you, Pups," and then he was off, out with his mates for an end-of-school party. And that was the last time Barry saw his son alive.

. . . . . . . . . . . . .

After a lively night out, Jimmy had come home in the early hours, found he had no door key and, rather than wake his family, climbed through an upstairs window and gone to bed. But to his mum's surprise, he was up bright and early the next day with a plan: being sixteen now and legally entitled, he was going to buy his first lottery ticket.

First things first, though – he was off to the Lee Café on Burnt Ash Road, with his older brother Tommy and a friend, for a full English fry-up. Not even winning the lottery could get in the way of breakfast. Tommy was eleven years older, stockier, shorter, and red-haired, while Jimmy was slim, tall, and dark, but there was no mistaking the same deep brown eyes, inherited from Margaret. Tommy worked as a builder, but music was his passion, and he had ambitions to travel; he was studying Mandarin and planning a trip to the Far East. In fact, he was off to a Mandarin class that morning and over breakfast was working on convincing his friend Antony to come with him. Still haggling, they popped next door to the betting shop, while Jimmy went home to quiz his mum about the lottery.

Margaret was in the front sitting room with Sammy T, Jimmy's 23-year-old sister, who has Down's syndrome. Samantha's unfailing Saturday morning ritual is to pitch camp in the front room after breakfast and watch the TV soaps till lunchtime. This morning, something on *Coronation Street* had caught Margaret's interest as she went back and forth, catching up on housework, and she'd perched on the edge of the sofa for a minute that had stretched to five and then ten. Jimmy wandered in.

"Jimmy came and sat beside me and said, 'Mum, I wanna do the lottery, now I'm sixteen,' and we were having a laugh, because I don't know much about it. He was asking me, 'Is it today, is it tomorrow? How do you do it?' I said, 'I don't really know, Jim. I think you can do a lucky jackpot or something, I don't know.' And then he went round the corner."

Off he'd gone, back round to the newsagent's, with his eighteen-year-old brother Harry this time, to try his luck. And that was the last time Margaret saw her son alive.

. . . . . . . . . . . . .

*My sister rang me to say, "I didn't see Jimmy on his birthday.[1] Please tell him I'm sorry I haven't sent his card." It's a standing joke in our house as we're always late with cards!*

*I said, "You know what he's like, he won't mind. They're all used to it."*

*"Wish him happy birthday for me?"*

1. For ease of understanding, throughout this book where Margaret is the narrator her words are set in italics.

*I said, "He's just gone round the corner. I'll tell him as soon as he comes back."*

*Then I went upstairs. I looked out of the bedroom window for some reason, and I saw a neighbour running into another neighbour's garden. I thought, "That's strange – why's Linda going into Eileen's garden?" Then I could hear my mobile phone going, which it doesn't very often. I ran downstairs to answer it, and it was my friend Eileen, yelling, "Margaret! Get round the corner quick! Jimmy's been attacked!"*

*And I ran. I grabbed my shoes, put them on, and started running. I felt like I was never going to get there, so I took them off and kept running, and as I got round the corner, I could see the baker's. There was all this commotion, and I'm thinking, "What on earth's going on?"*

*Then I saw Harry, bent over, and Tommy's friend Anthony standing with him, and I'm thinking, "Where's Jimmy?" And I ran in the baker's, and I didn't have my shoes on. There was glass all over the floor, and everyone's screaming, "Put your shoes on, there's glass!"*

*So I did, and I'm screaming back, "Where's Jimmy? Where's Jimmy?"*

*And they're all screaming back at me, "Don't go out the back, don't go out the back!"*

*"Don't tell me what to do!" I remember saying it so clearly. "Don't tell me what to do! Where's Jimmy?"*

*And as I went out the back, there was Jimmy, lying in a pool of blood, in Tommy's arms. My first thought was, "What's Tommy doing here?" – because I didn't know. I didn't even know Harry had gone round the corner, but they're adults; I don't have to know what they're doing. Then Tommy said to me, "Mum, go out, go out, it's going to be OK."*

*It sounds silly, but my first thought was that he'd had his ear cut off.*

*Then I fainted.*

．．．．．．．．．．．．．

"I was studying Mandarin at the time," Tommy recalls. "I was getting ready to go to my lessons. I was persuading a friend of mine to come up to town with me and hang around while I did it, and then we'd go and do something together afterwards. He said he would, so I hung around for an extra ten minutes, waiting for the next train.

"Then I got a phone call from Harry, saying someone was starting some trouble with Jimmy, come round the corner. He didn't actually say where he was. He just said that they were in trouble, so my initial reaction was to run round. I had my bag on my back, 'cause I was ready to go. So I ran. It felt like it took a long time to run round, like something was holding me back from running as fast as I could. Maybe it was the thought in my head that something bad had happened. I got round and got to the crossing, where a neighbour was standing, and she said, 'Jimmy's in trouble.'

"I ran straight across the road in front of all the cars and came to the chemist, just before the bakery, and everyone's shouting, 'What's going on?' I know one guy said something to me, but I can't remember what he said. He turned out to be the guy who was in the bakery as well, with them.

"Just as I got halfway past the pharmacy, a guy runs out of the bakery – I instantly assumed this was the guy who'd done something, because he ran in such a way, and then I saw Harry standing at the door as I ran past. So I chased this guy. He was clearly faster than I was – most people are, unfortunately. I probably ran about 10 metres away from the bakery. I knew I couldn't catch him. I screamed out a lot of things – I said I'd kill him when I found him. At this point I didn't know what had happened, but it's just an instant reaction, if someone messes with one of your family.

"Then something clicked in my head: I hadn't seen Jimmy. I saw Harry – he was standing outside the bakery – but I didn't see Jimmy. I knew the guy had been picking on Jimmy. So I ran back into the bakery. It all went into slow motion. As I ran in, I can picture everything perfectly. I remember seeing the glass – one of the glass panes from the door was kicked in. That was the first thing I saw: broken glass everywhere, and sausages, and then traces of blood. They started off small and got bigger and bigger. I ran round behind the counter, and I was saying to the girls, 'Where is he? Where's Jimmy?'

"They were screaming frantically, and they yelled, 'He's out the back!' So I went back there – I was literally following a trail of blood – to a cupboard, where the door had blood on the handle. I remember grabbing the handle and pulling the door. I thought it was locked at first. I pulled it harder, and Jim was on the other side, holding the handle, like he was trying to stop someone coming in. I remember shouting, 'It's me, Jim! It's Tommy!' He let go of the door and it swung open, but he came with the door.

"I remember that moment – I looked at his face. I guess it was the last point where he actually could notice anyone was there. It was an odd look. It was like... scared, but also happy that I was there. It was such a horrible look. I remember looking in his eyes – it must have been a second, no more than that – and then looking at his neck and seeing the blood coming out. I think that was when he fainted into my arms."

. . . . . . . . . . . . .

"I'd gone to work before Jimmy had got up," Barry recalls. "I'd given him a day off, because of his birthday. I'd gone in the shop; we opened at nine. I have one person who works with me, called Mark. We're working away, it's a bit quiet at the start, and then we had a really difficult customer come in. Something was not right with the shoes, or whatever. In the end, I thought, 'This woman's being incredibly difficult; trying to turn us over.' First she couldn't find her ticket, then she did but the shoes had gone missing – clearly she'd had them and come back with different tickets!

"I was having a bad morning. It's strange how these things go. We're working away, and it's getting towards midday. The machines are all going, and it starts to get busy, servicing of shoes going back and forth. Then the phone went, the landline. By the time I'd got out there, it had gone. So I quickly pressed 1471, but didn't recognize the number and left it. So next thing, it's gone again. This time, I've got to it and it's Margaret, screaming down the phone. 'Barry! Get to the baker's quick! Jimmy's been attacked and it looks bad.'

"I threw the shop keys at Mark and yelled what had happened and dashed off to the van. Mark knew Jimmy, because they'd worked together, and he loved talking about computer games with him. He had a lot of time for Jimmy. I'd parked about a quarter of a mile away, and I run there, I get in the van, I'm driving and I'm praying, 'Lord, God, let him be all right, please. Please, God, let him be all right.' Something inside, you know, it's almost as though... well, you don't know what's coming.

"I got towards the area, just off the South Circular, and the main road leading down to the baker's is blocked off. I'm thinking, 'Lord, what's going on?' You feel worse and worse all the time. I've done a U-turn, gone back again round the back road, and I'm coming down the side road, next to the bakery. A lady I knew, who lives a hundred yards from the corner, was standing outside looking... You're aware of people everywhere... I drove my van straight into her driveway. 'Vera,' I says, 'it's my son. It's Jimmy.' I gave her the keys and ran."

· · · · · · · · · · · ·

"There were so many people behind me, screaming, 'Do this, do that,'" Tommy recalls. "I remember screaming at everyone, 'Get the ambulance, get the police, get me tissues!' At the same time, I was talking to Jim – at every stage I didn't stop talking to him. Someone passed me a big load of J-cloths. I was putting them on his neck to try and stop the blood coming out, and it wasn't working. Then I had a load of blue roll, trying to soak it up, and that wasn't stopping it coming out. I didn't want to move him, because I could see the cut, and I was worried that I'd do more damage, so I just left him in position. He was basically breathing in his own blood at that point, as it was everywhere, all over me. It was an odd feeling: I felt like I was in two places at once. I was talking to all these people, but at the same time I was in this little bubble with Jimmy that no one else could get into. I remember saying to him that he'd be all right, that he'd wake up tomorrow and we'd all be laughing about it and having fun like we always do. And I was telling him, if I find the guy who did this, I'll kill him...

"Mum walked in halfway through, and she wanted to see him, and I said, 'No, he's fine, Mum, you don't need to... you don't need to come and see him, I'll look after him.' But I felt later she should have been there with him. I always felt bad about that. It's something I regret doing.

"I think I remember the point where I realized he was dead. It was odd because it hit me that he'd stopped breathing. I realized then, 'Oh my God, he's dead!' There was something in my head telling me not to believe that: 'No, no, that's not real. He must still be alive, that can't be happening, it doesn't happen, shouldn't happen to people, good people, we can save him, people do miracles these days…' I kept trying to get him to breathe, talking to him: 'I'm still here, the paramedics are coming, they'll save you, it's fine,' but I think, deep down, I knew. He'd literally stopped breathing and he was making this horrible, gargling noise, the sound you make when you take your last breath.

"Then the paramedics turned up, and I remember saying, 'They're here now, you'll be fine,' and the police were saying, 'You have to get out now,' and they dragged me out. That was the last time I saw him. I remember walking outside and seeing Harry, so I said, 'What happened?' I think he was in a state of shock. He couldn't talk; he was shaking. And people started arriving, family members, friends – everyone was appearing and saying, 'What's going on?' I thought, 'I've no idea. This shouldn't be happening to our family.'

"Because I was the last one with him, everyone's asking me, 'Is he all right? What's going on?' And I'm saying, 'He's fine, he'll be fine.' I knew that he wasn't. I just felt I had to tell everyone that he was. I was too afraid to say it to everyone. You want to give people hope."

. . . . . . . . . . . .

*I'm not a weak person. I don't know why I fainted. As I came round, someone in the shop lent me their mobile phone. I phoned Barry and I screamed, "Jimmy's been attacked in the baker's and it looks bad: get down here quick!" Then I went outside, and by that time my friend Eileen had come round. She used to be a nurse, so I dragged her in, saying, "Quick, quick, come and see what you can do!" She went out to Jimmy and it was chaos then. I can hear the voices – there's a chap from another shop on the phone in the baker's, phoning the paramedics. I could hear him saying, "He's not breathing. Why are you not here yet? We called you a while ago!"*

*Then the paramedics were there and we were ushered out of the shop. Tommy came out and he was covered in blood. I remember him sitting on the grass, and I remember Harry, poor Harry… Then we were phoning people: I phoned my daughter Joanne, and her boyfriend answered, and I said, "Andy, Jimmy's been attacked and it looks bad."*

*It must have been half an hour before Barry turned up, or an hour. It felt like it was minutes, pacing around, waiting for the paramedics to come out and tell us what was happening. There was a policewoman there and I said, "I need to contact my son, he's in Spain." Danny was in Spain on a rugby tour. And the next thing, I can see Barry running down the road. I was rushing up to him and just as I did, the paramedics came out. We ran up to them and they took their gloves off and one of them said, "He's dead."*

*I think I fainted again. Our youngest son George was outside by then, and he burst into tears. Joanne took him into the back of the ambulance and said to him, "Don't worry, Jimmy's gone to heaven."*

*George stopped crying, and he hasn't cried since.He was only eight.*

*Those words – "He's gone to heaven…" This quiet descended over everyone. The whole place went quiet.*

# 2

# What Happened?

A Saturday edition of *The Sun*, a couple of bottles of Coke, a small packet of chewing gum, spotted with dried blood, and a lottery ticket dated 10 May 2008. The last items Jimmy ever bought now sit in a sealed plastic bag in a cupboard in the Mizen family home. They have no use; they have not been shaped into a memorial or a shrine, but they cannot be thrown away. The sealed bag is like a time capsule, preserving some of the strangely inconsequential relics of what happened that Saturday morning, the lottery ticket a poignant reminder of what we call chance – how things might so easily have gone otherwise.

· · · · · · · · · · · · ·

After the newsagent's, Harry popped into the Three Cooks Bakery to pick up a snack, as he did every Saturday morning, Jimmy with him. There were two women working behind the counter, the manager Lesley Crocker and her sixteen-year-old assistant Samantha, and one customer, a man in his late forties. As Harry and Jimmy waited by the counter to be served, another teenager entered the bakery. He was short, wiry, and aggressive, his swarthy face framed with the goatee beard, sideburns, and gold earrings of a would-be rapper. He strutted up and down, complaining loudly to the staff in his "gangsta" patois, demanding to know why there were no chicken sandwiches left. Heading for the cake counter, he found his way blocked by Jimmy and Harry, waiting patiently to be served. He tried to barge past, but Jimmy, a whole head taller, stood his ground.

"Get out the fuckin' way!" spat the newcomer.

Jimmy turned and looked down to meet his gaze. "Some manners wouldn't go amiss," he said quietly.

"What?" The little guy was glowering in disbelief. No one spoke to him like this. He was respected. He was someone. He was Dirrty Detz, gangsta rapper, drug dealer, street-fighter. This kid didn't know who he was dealing with.

"What the fuck you say?"

Unruffled by all the menace and swagger, Jimmy replied calmly, "Say please and I might move."

That was it. A torrent of fury burst forth: "You think you're a big man, huh? Think you're better than me? Think you're a big man? I'll show you how big you are! Fuckin' step outside, I'll show you how fuckin' big you are…"

Harry stepped forward, attempting to calm things down. "All right," he said, "there's no need for any trouble."

"Trouble? You fuckin' step outside and I'll give you trouble. I'll give you a fuckin' slap, both of you!"

"All right, that's enough," said the manager, "you get out now." Still seething, the angry youth flounced out and paced and postured up and down the pavement. "You get out here! Hey, you! Big man! Get out here and I'll fuckin' show you!"

Harry was on his phone now, calling his older brother Tommy: "Get round here quick, Tom, there's a problem, someone starting on Jimmy in the Three Cooks…"

Seeing him on the phone, the little bully stormed back into the shop, with renewed outrage. "Who the fuck you callin'? Huh? Grassin' me up, huh?"

"Look, they don't want to know." The other customer, the older man, had stepped in front of him now, trying to reason with him. "Just leave it, OK?"

Now what? Who did this guy think he was, trying to interfere? The boy shoved his face menacingly in the older man's and hissed, "You don't know who you're dealing with." A few days before, in his Dirrty Detz persona, he'd recorded a series of raps on a friend's phone, boasting about his criminal lifestyle, listing the different types of super-strength skunk cannabis he could supply, and proclaiming himself to be a "top shotter", a big-time drug dealer. "He was getting through some serious weed," a former friend said later, "and becoming increasingly paranoid and unpredictable."

The older man was backing away, and Dirrty Detz was past him and renewing his verbal assault on Harry. "Fuckin' grassin' me up, eh?" the rant continued, "Wait a minute, I remember you…"

Harry had recognized this guy several minutes ago; there was history between them. He was not Dirrty Detz the gangster rapper; his name was Jake Fahri, son of Mustafa and Shirley Fahri, and they lived nearby. He was the same age as Harry, and seven years previously, when they were both twelve, attending different schools in Eltham, Jake had mugged Harry and stolen his sweets and some loose change. After ignoring an initial complaint from Harry's parents, Jake's school was obliged to respond when the deputy head of Harry's school, St Thomas More, made contact. Crown Woods School gave assurances that Jake had been spoken to, that he was very sorry, and it wouldn't happen again. Two years later, Jake had recognized Harry as he stepped off the bus in Burnt Ash Hill and attacked him again, punching and kicking him in the chest and stomach. A neighbour who witnessed the attack brought Harry home.

"He was distraught," Barry recalls. "Your heart bleeds. Harry wasn't the kind of boy to retaliate." This time the Mizens went to the police. Several weeks later, officers sat in the Mizens' front room assuring Margaret and Barry that they had visited the Fahri family, spoken with Jake and his parents, that everyone was very, very sorry and it wouldn't happen again…

The following year, 2004, Jake was given a nine-month referral order for robbing a schoolboy at knifepoint with a gang in Bexley. Within six months, he had added to this a twelve-month supervision order for the assault and robbery of a man in Greenwich Park, and just over a year later, in April 2006, further offences of burglary and common assault on a sixteen-year-old girl earned him an additional eighteen-month supervision order. In February 2007, his trial at

Camberwell Youth Court for the alleged rape of a thirteen-year-old girl the previous year was discontinued after the girl withdrew her evidence, apparently unable to face the ordeal of going to court.

So this was the angry youth parading up and down in front of Jimmy and Harry, screaming and swearing at them to fight, and now jabbing his car key in their faces to provoke them. Still they refused to react. Enraged by their seeming indifference, Jake grabbed a couple of large plastic drink bottles from the cooler and laid into Jimmy and Harry, beating them repeatedly around their heads, ears, shoulders, necks, wherever he could reach.

At last the brothers responded. Together they shoved Jake backwards, sending him crashing into the cake counter, smashing one of the glass panels, and then pummelled and pushed him towards the exit, forcing him out onto the pavement. They shut the bakery doors on him and held them firm from the inside. The young assistant was calling the police from the back of the shop.

Outside, onlookers were beginning to gather, drawn by raised voices and the noise of the fight. Jake didn't care. As one of the witnesses later described, he'd gone berserk. "You fuckin' cowards!" he bawled, hopping this way and that in paroxysms of fury. Screaming and raving, he grabbed hold of a metal advertising sign on the pavement, with a heavy concrete base, and swung it with all his force into the glass doors. A shower of glass exploded across the shop floor as the brothers fell back, horrified. Jake rammed his way through the broken doors, dragging the metal sign, and went after Jimmy, pursuing him round behind the counter and swinging the concrete base at him like a cudgel. Jimmy caught the sign and tried to wrestle it off Jake, but he'd never encountered such a rabid frenzy of violence. Deprived of one weapon, Jake's sharpened instinct for mayhem immediately spotted another.

Dropping the sign, he grabbed a Pyrex dish full of sausages from the hotplate, hoisted it in both hands to shoulder height and hurled it up into Jimmy's face with maximum strength. An explosion of glass fragments, hot sausages and spattering fat burst between them as Jimmy reeled from the impact. A fountain of blood erupted from his neck, up and out in a glistening red slick through the air, across the counter, the floor, the ceiling, showering the shop manager in a warm spray as she cowered against the wall. "Like a scene from a horror film," she would say later, those three? four? five? seconds while she screamed, eyes wide with horror, as the old oven dish split apart against Jimmy's chin like a nail-bomb, shattering razor-edged shards into his neck, stabbing deep, slicing veins and arteries, and driving on to bury themselves in his spine.

Now Jimmy was staggering, clutching his neck, and Jake was fleeing, darting out from behind the counter, and out of the shop, running down the road with a smirk on his face. As Harry stood stunned in the doorway, and the women screamed in horror, Jimmy was stumbling away, leaking blood across the floor as he dragged himself into a storage cupboard out at the back of the shop.

Terrified and bewildered by Jake's onslaught, and the sight of his own blood flooding out all over himself, Jimmy focused all his departing consciousness on retreating to some place of refuge and defending himself from further attacks. But, with both his carotid artery and jugular vein severed, the boy trembling in the dark cupboard, clinging to the door handle in terror, hands slippery with blood, had only minutes to live.

Jimmy had started the last day of his life by buying his first lottery ticket. From start to finish, the senseless assault that robbed him of his life had lasted just three minutes.

# 3

# Margaret's Journey

*I was born in Greenwich, in south-east London, in August 1952. My parents lived just two roads from the hospital where I was born. Apart from my dad, we were all Catholics; we went to the local Catholic school and church, together with our cousins on my mum's side, and generally lived a very Christian way of life. We went to Mass on Sundays (if not it was a sin, and we would be in trouble with the parish priest, Father Pepper), and on Wednesdays we went to Mass with the school.*

*As a very little girl I used to wonder why my mum never took Holy Communion, but I gradually became aware that in fact she had been married before, and the church would not accept divorcees. This troubled me because I was rather a sensitive soul, and I knew it hurt my mum not to be able to have the Holy Sacrament. In that way the Catholic Church now is so very different. If one feels unable to take Holy Communion for some reason, then it is fine to have a blessing from the priest, and this can be very rewarding in itself. Dad, though, was very supportive of our religion and went along with everything that was asked of him in that way, never questioning it.*

*We had a very contented family life, and I feel I had a happy childhood. I am not saying my parents didn't argue from time to time, but they were never big arguments. Dad was a painter and decorator, working for a company called Johnson & Philips. It was there that he met my mum, when she worked in the staff canteen. When Dad was about forty years old, he fell from a ladder and broke his hip and was hospitalized for a long period of time. Legend has it that I pined terribly for my dad during that time and I kept getting ill, resulting finally in a nasty bout of pneumonia. As soon as my dad heard this, he immediately discharged himself from the hospital, which made his own recovery even more difficult. I, of course, got better. Dad was unable to continue with his manual work after his accident, but I believe it gave him* the impetus to go on an accountancy course, something he had always had an interest in and a tremendous aptitude for. He sailed through the course at Holborn College with flying colours.He was lucky enough to get a job straight away and he eventually became the chief accountant for Dillon's University Bookshop, which was attached to London University in Malet Street, and we were all very proud of him.

Mum had several jobs to help keep the family going during Dad's incapacity and indeed his studying. She worked as a waitress at the Maritime Museum restaurant and then was a ward orderly in the Seamen's Hospital. Mum worked there for many years, up until she retired really. It was a lovely place, a beautiful old building with lots of history, and she used to take me to work with her sometimes, and I got to know the Matron, who used to make a fuss of me. Mum worked really hard; I remember her being up at half six, and Dad seeing her off to work, and then she'd be home by one o'clock, and when we came home from school the house would be warm and cosy, there'd be a big roaring fire in the hearth, and our comics (which we loved) would be out ready for us, and by six o'clock there would always be a delicious dinner on the table.

We didn't have fancy holidays (in those days most people didn't go abroad); it was always a caravan or a chalet at the seaside or staying with relatives somewhere, but when Dad eventually received compensation for his accident we went to a beautiful Butlins hotel in Cliftonville. I remember it clearly because I was seven years old and I won a junior beauty competition, Miss Junior Lovely! My sister and I wanted badly to go in the swimming pool, but neither of us could swim and it was 8 foot deep all round. So we worried our dad to take us in, and we nagged and nagged him until he relented. He came down in his swimming trunks and took the plunge; he went under and it seemed like he wasn't going to come back up. We started screaming, and a couple of people were poised to dive in and save him when he suddenly surfaced and was absolutely fine. He said to us to come on in with him (with our water wings on), but we were having none of it. Nothing could persuade us. So poor Dad nearly drowned for nothing!

We lived in a pleasant street called Annandale Road, where we had a beautiful big garden, with steam trains and even double-decker trains going past the fence at the end of the garden. We had wonderful neighbours *everywhere, whose children were our friends.It was a lovely, friendly, cosy life in Annandale Road, just off the very steep Vanbrugh Hill, which leads up to Blackheath. Dad used to walk us up to the ponds at Blackheath to watch the boats on Sundays while Mum cooked a lovely roast.*

*We had lots of friends in the street, and I have never forgotten them, although we have mostly lost touch. My best girlfriend was called Sandy Ford and my best boyfriend was Peter Morris. I was convinced I would marry Peter when I grew up. We used to talk about it all the time and have play marriages.*

*Then, when I was about eight, we were informed that our house (along with most of our friends' houses) was going to be properly converted into council flats, so we moved to a council estate in West Greenwich. West Greenwich at the time was not the trendy place it is now. I actually felt quite terrorized there. I was constantly bullied, although I kept it to myself, as victims of bullies so often do. The only time I felt safe was inside with my family. I was a quiet, sensitive child and I really couldn't come to terms with leaving our beautiful Victorian house with its huge garden and all our lovely friends to live in this awful place. I never said anything to my parents, for fear of upsetting them, but I do sometimes wonder, in hindsight, why Mum and Dad accepted that flat. Maybe they thought they had no choice. I don't know. Maybe they didn't have a choice. I never asked them, even in later years.*

*I remember us all being quite excited to be moving. It was the mindset of the times to be excited about moving into a flat with all mod cons, as they would say, not realizing what it would turn out to be like. I did make some friends, of course, and the warmth and love of our family home was always there, but when we moved from there to Hither Green, when I was fifteen, it was the biggest joy of my life!*

*I struggled with my schoolwork, both at primary school and at secondary school. I don't know why. I seemed to be well liked by the teachers and I never misbehaved. All the teachers would chat to me, and I was a bit of a teacher's pet, but academically I was a no-no! In hindsight, once again, and with my experience now, I would say that I probably needed extra support with school work, but in those days things weren't quite the same. A lot of children were allowed to muddle through in the same way. I had a couple of close friends at school.One was called Raphael. She had a bad heart, so was always very weak and eventually very sadly passed away after anappendix operation.*

Another friend had only one leg, having been in a car accident. I have always been drawn to people with problems.

I don't remember having religion forced upon us at home. We all knew our religious duties from school. Mum always said, "We're good Catholics." We said our morning and night prayers because we wanted to. We gave up something for Lent (usually sweets!), and on Fridays we didn't eat meat. My dad would drop us off at church every Sunday, and Mum would sometimes come too, although not very often for fear of condemnation because of her divorce. It was like that in those days – she believed she was excommunicated.

Although we were always being told off for giggling in church, I always knew that I believed. I never questioned it. Once, when I was staying with a young friend, when I was about six or seven, I woke up in the night and I was convinced I saw a vision of God. I can still see that vision in my mind: a recognizable image of Jesus, with long hair and a beard. Maybe it was just the outline of a shadow, but I still feel, when I think back to it, that I saw God. From a very young age, maybe three or four, I always thought that God had this big black book in heaven. When your name was written in it, your time was up, and you'd go up to heaven. That's how I still feel: we have no say in it when our time is up. If God is ready for us, that's it. I was always a bit scared of doing something naughty (which is not to say I never did), because I didn't want God to get upset with me. I spent a good deal of my youth praying, presumably because of my Catholic conscience.

My family called me Marny, or Marny-Potts (my brother still does), so it was always little Marny-Potts tagging along behind my sister and her friends. I'm sure I got on their nerves, but they never complained. Although I was only two years younger, my sister always seemed rather more grown up and "streetwise" than I was and always tried to keep me sheltered from the outside world. As we were growing up, it was always Elizabeth and Margaret, Lynny and Marny-Potts, Lyn and Marn, and to our family we still are Lyn and Marn. She has always been my best friend. My sister loved the Beatles and all the Sixties bands, and it proved to be her educational downfall, or so it seemed. She ended up getting expelled from the grammar school for playing truant so often to go and see them. I was quieter, being happy to stay at home and watch the TV, read my comics and books, and stay in with my mum and dad.

*During those years we had lots of people around us: any relative or even friends who needed a roof over their heads when in difficulty would come and stay temporarily. Dad's brother, Uncle Stan, lived with us after my grandmother died in 1958 until he got married in 1966 – he was a real character, a painter and decorator. He always made us laugh.*

*My mum's brother, my Uncle Tom, also stayed with us from time to time with his wife and children. They lived in Wales, in Swansea, but he was a stone mason and sometimes had to follow where the work was. Sometimes he came on his own. But my memory is of all of them coming and going, and we had lots of fun. They had two children, albino twins, Dawn and Diane, and we were all very close. Their mother was an alcoholic. The drinking culture in Wales then seemed to be for women to only go out to the pub on Friday and Saturday nights, and that would be it. But it got more and more until eventually, in later life, she was drinking at home as well – not necessarily very much, but when you're an alcoholic, one or two drinks can tip you over the edge.*

*The twins had white, curly hair, almost Afro, and white skin and pink eyes; people used to stare, and it was very hard for them. They came up to London because of my uncle's work and stayed for some years, but eventually went back to Swansea. The twins both died within five years of each other, tragically only in their twenties. This broke their parents' hearts. My aunt died not long afterwards, and Uncle Tom, although he still visited London regularly for work, could not make the move back to London permanently because they were all buried in Swansea. He couldn't bring himself to leave them. As broken-hearted as he was, though, he had a most fantastic sense of humour and a kind and loving demeanour and used to make us all laugh. We loved him very much. He died following an accident in Swansea and was buried with his family.*

*My dad had four brothers and four sisters living nearby, and they were all very close, and my parents were very welcoming and always hospitable, so we always had a houseful. This was reciprocated and my memories of my aunts and uncles and cousins on both sides and the parties and the happy family life are very precious to me.*

*I still consider Greenwich home, or let's say when I go to Greenwich I feel a sense of coming home. Mum and Dad went through a phase of visiting the local pubs when we were in our teens, and as we became old enough we would sometimes go with them. Afterwards Dad would take us all to a restaurant and treat us to a lovely meal. It's a wonderful place, Greenwich, breathtakingly beautiful, with its park, the river, and the historic buildings. The river walkway is still exactly the same as when we were young, and to go there now is like taking a step back in time. I wouldn't want it to change.*

*It's very trendy now, but it wasn't in those days. It was a traditional London suburb, and Saturday was pie and mash day. All the houses, which were nothing special back then, are now worth a lot of money! I've got to know some of the children from my old school, through the London Citizens network, and it's great to reminisce. In those young days we spent so much time in Greenwich Park – we took it for granted because it was on our doorstep, but it was marvellous to go there and play, visit the museum (daily in the holidays), and take a boat out on the little boating pond.*

*My brother used to take us to school in the mornings, one by one on the back of his bike. If my mum had known, she would have had a fit! She was always frightened of the roads because my sister had an accident at the age of only three, when she darted across the road in front of a van and broke her leg in three places. I suppose it could have been a lot worse, but Mum was never the same afterwards. My mum used to walk through the Greenwich Market every day to the Seamen's Hospital. When President Kennedy was shot, my mum and I were shopping in the little supermarket (the first one I ever knew) called Bass's, near the market, and I remember the news coming on the radio in the shop.*

*If Mum and Dad went out for a drink at the weekends, they'd sometimes quarrel when they came home. Mum used to say, "When the drink's in, the wit's out." I can remember having my head under the pillow if they argued, I hated it. I was terribly sensitive. But always the next day, they'd be dancing around the room together, and I'd be so happy. When Dad died in 1995, it felt a bit like the end of the world, because it was so sudden, and he was such a wonderful father. He loved all of us so much and would do absolutely anything for us. He was brought up in a large family himself, and his father had died at the age of only forty-five. It was incumbent upon him thereafter to look after his family and his mother. This really set the scene for the rest of his life. He was always a tower of strength to all, as was our mum, and I know if they had been around when Jimmy died, they would have been such tremendous support, even in their own grief.*

*I was aware of people's needs from an early age. My nan used to say I had more feeling in my little finger than all her other grandchildren put together! I'm not sure if that's true, but she did say it. I remember feeling things deeply, and I was always attracted to the more vulnerable people as I always felt I could help them. I think my awareness of other people's needs sometimes causes me more grief than maybe it should. I worry if someone seems to be left out of any situation; I feel it's my job to make sure everyone's included. I hate for anyone to feel hurt or left out and I try very hard to ensure it doesn't happen. I have a large family and they all have their own lives, and inevitably this can sometimes happen.*

*From quite a young age, I was always looking after someone, and children were my passion, which eventually led to my job as a nanny.*

. . . . . . . . . . . . .

*I left school a week before my fifteenth birthday. You could leave at fifteen in those days, andas I wasn't academic in any way at all I had no intention of staying on. My first job was working in an office, at the Park Lane Hotel in Piccadilly, but I wasn't cut out for it. I had to keep the books for the hairdressing department and I was always adding the columns up wrongly and being called into the manager's office. I couldn't take much more of the stress and thought I would change my job as soon as I could. I saw an advert in the local paper for a job as a nanny so I applied for it and was taken on.*

*The job was to look after a family of five boys, sons of a local curate and his wife, Francis and Anne Gardom, who were from a very upper-class background. I absolutely loved my work; I became very close to the children, and the work never felt like a chore. Every day I took the children to Greenwich Park, which was only about a hundred yards away from the Gardoms' house. It wasn't well paid, but money didn't mean an awful lot to me; I had enough to get by and go out once a week with my sister. I probably gave my mum some money too. I remember my brother saying to me, "You look after all these children; you'll never want children of your own," but that couldn't have been further from the truth. I worked for the Gardoms during the week, and sometimes during my holidays I would get requests to care for other children* whose parents wanted to go away on their own for the weekend, or suchlike. I was quite young, only seventeen or eighteen, but the families seemed to trust me and I tried never to let them down.

I did have a bit of a social life. My sister and I used to love going dancing at the Royal Artillery Barracks in Woolwich; I remember that we went every Tuesday and I actually got engaged to a soldier! It didn't last very long, a few months or so, and then I decided that it wasn't right. He was a lovely chap, from Huddersfield, but he was due to be posted abroad, and I was only sixteen. I couldn't up and leave my job. It was very important to me.

When I was eighteen, I was temporarily working for a family in Upper Norwood who were going skiing for a couple of weeks and they wanted me to look after their children. While I was staying there, the children's uncle, their father's brother Brendan, arrived from Canada. He was actually Australian and he was travelling round the world, as many Australians did, and so when he was passing through London, he wanted to stay at his brother's house. He was six or seven years older than me, and while I was cooking a meal for him, he told me a lot of fascinating stories about all his glamorous adventures. I was impressed, certainly, and he was very charming. I'd said goodnight and gone to bed and was reading a book for a bit before going to sleep, and he came upstairs and came into my room and, well, one thing led to another. I thought I was passionately in love – for about a day – but it was perfectly clear that he wasn't interested beyond a one-night stand, and off he went, back to Australia.

I didn't know I was pregnant until seven months had gone by. I hadn't put on weight, but as I was always slightly overweight, my large tummy was normal for me. I began to have an inkling because of movement in my tummy, so I went to the doctor and he said, yes, you're thirty-two weeks pregnant! I really didn't expect it. I was a stay-at-home, quiet kind of girl, and it was to prove quite a surprise for many people who knew me. The "Swinging Sixties" seemed to have passed me by, and here I was, having a baby, in two months' time! Because of my quiet kind of life, taking precautions would never have entered my head. I know I had that one slip-up with Brendan, but that seemed like ages ago, and I had no intentions of ever slipping up again. I remember the doctor saying, "You're too late for an abortion." I was absolutely horrified at the very idea of an abortion anyway. No, I would have this baby. I adored children and I wanted this baby.

*I didn't know how to tell my parents. But I didn't have much time to lose – they would have to be told. Strangely, my sister says she had looked at me one day and thought to herself that I looked pregnant sideways. Then she thought "No, not possible with Marn, she doesn't have a boyfriend and never goes out." But she did ask me, funnily enough, around the time I did find out. Of course, I had to admit it to her. For a couple of days she kept saying that I would have to tell Mum and Dad. She remembers saying to me, "What will you do, then, just walk in with a baby in your arms one day?" And I said, "Yes."*

*My sister told them for me one night, when it was just she and my mum still up. Mum had an initial fit! Dad, strangely, did not turn a hair. They both came into the bedroom where I was in bed but awake, and Dad said, "Don't worry, love, we are here for you. We will look after you." And that is exactly what they did. The negative soon turned into the positive. We were all looking forward to the birth of our new baby, and she would be loved, adored, and cherished. Clothes were bought, and all the necessary equipment. Mum and Dad were looking forward to having another grandchild (they already had two, Karen and Richard, my brother's first two children).*

*My sister says she remembers me going into labour with Joanne. We shared a bedroom and I told her it was starting. She says the very first thing I did was get out of bed and wash my hair, as if that was important, at the same time groaning every time there was another contraction. And strangely (it must be vanity) I have always done exactly the same thing ever since. With each child, I wouldn't go into hospital without washing my hair!*

*The ambulance came, and as I arrived at the hospital, a nurse said to me, "When you leave this hospital, you'll be leaving with a baby." I thought, "Wow!" Mum had to go to work and then came to be with me at lunchtime. She was there when Joanne was born. That was very special. So I had my beautiful baby girl, and visitors started arriving. It was lovely, the most wonderful thing. I remember holding Joanne up and looking at her – at how bonny and beautiful she was, and thanking God for giving her to me. I remember all my family leaving, and holding my baby up at the window for them all to see. My precious baby girl – Joanne Elizabeth.*

*I wrote to Joanne's father, Brendan Fagan, to let him know. I thought I needed to tell him that he had a daughter. I made it clear that I didn't want or expect anything from him, just his acknowledgment that my child was his. There was no reply, so I wrote again, and this time he sent a letter back. I remember it word for word: "Dear Margaret, thank you for the letter, glad your parents are well. I'm coming to Europe sometime next year. Until then, I'd prefer if you didn't write." And that was it.*

*When I think about it, it was so cold. It didn't upset me because he was a lost love, but because he was the father of my lovely little girl. I thought she so deserved to be acknowledged. Then again, sometimes I think, "Would I really have wanted him to be part of her life?" I don't know. It's a terribly complicated situation. One has to ask oneself, is the seed that made the baby really important, in a situation like this? Surely the people who bring up the baby are more important. But of course, in the eyes of the law, the seed is important. As many adopted children well know, finding out where you come from is sometimes a lifetime's work, and the desire to know this can be all-consuming. Anyway, I didn't hear from him again and he eventually more or less drifted from my mind.*

*In the Catholic Church it is important to have a baby baptized early, the earlier the better. So when Joanne was twelve days old, I went straight to my parish priest and arranged her baptism. She was born on 25 November 1971 and baptized just before Christmas. The priest knew I wasn't married. He was a kindly priest and didn't seem to judge me, and for that matter I never felt anyone judging me. On the contrary, I felt everyone loved us both, me and my child. Certainly my family completely doted on Jo, and she was surrounded by love and affection; we both were. Mum and Dad adored her, my sister wouldn't let the wind blow on her, and Joanne's arrival just enriched our lives. There is always, of course, a stigma attached to having a child out of wedlock, and if I am honest, being a Catholic, I did sometimes feel guilty from a "sinning" point of view. But then I would think that God would never have considered it a sin for me to bring this little person into the world, and I satisfied my conscience with that.*

*After Joanne was born, I carried on looking after the Gardom children, taking her to work with me much of the time. I also still stayed with other families who needed me from time to time, and managed to juggle work with being a mum.*

*I had actually planned to travel, the following year. I'd answered an advertisement in* The Times. *A group of young people were travelling round* the world and looking for one more to make up the numbers, and I'd written in and been accepted. I couldn't do that now, of course, but the Gardoms, who had known about the planned travelling, seemed relieved, because they apparently didn't want to lose me! They were the kindest people to work for and they completely accepted me taking my baby to work with me. I know they absolutely trusted me with the care of their little boys, and we all had a happy relationship. Of course it was ideal for me, and although as their boys got older my work for them gradually eased off, we remained firm friends and I kept in touch with them for many years.

From the council flat in Greenwich we had actually moved to a very pleasant house in Hither Green. I loved Hither Green. It was a completely different area for us, but we soon felt very much at home. We loved it. We lived there when I had Joanne. It was where I would eventually meet Barry, my husband, and the house we moved to is actually just around the corner from our coffee shop, the Café of Good Hope.

. . . . . . . . . . . . .

On a very rare Saturday night out with my sister and her friends to the Lyceum in the Strand, I met a young man called Alan. He was a very pleasant chap and we started going out together and eventually got engaged. But deep down inside I knew he wasn't really the one for me. Although he was a good man, I wasn't madly in love with him, but I allowed the relationship to drift on. I knew that I had to tell him one day, but I wanted it to evolve gently and not be a shock to him.

We were still seeing each other when I met Barry. This was a couple of years later, when I went out one evening for a drink with a couple of friends. At this time I was working evenings in various theatres in the West End, and Barry, who had a shop around the corner from my home, had started walking to the station with me every evening. Actually (and unbeknown to him) I timed it so that my walk to the station coincided with him closing his shop, and as he had to pass through the station to get home, we casually walked together. I was still seeing Alan, but it didn't stop me liking Barry. At this point, though, we were just chatting on the way to the train, and in all honesty I didn't think I had a chance.

On this one particular evening, however, I was in the pub with my friends and there he was, the object of my big crush, and I couldn't believe my luck.

We were chatting as usual, and this time he walked me home afterwards from the pub, and from then on we were together. I remember telling my sister, "You'll never guess – I went to the pub last night, and guess who was there?" She guessed straight away who it was. I always spoke of him. Our romance started, and I told Alan as soon as I could. He was very upset, and of course I was very sorry for that. I think I probably broke his heart at the time, but with Barry it was the real thing; he swept me off my feet. I really did know that this was it.

It was a real whirlwind romance, and within a short time we'd booked the wedding at the local Catholic Church: St Saviour's in Lewisham. We were married within a year. Thirty-five years on, I still feel as much in love as ever. If I see Barry out and about somewhere, I still get flutters in my tummy!

I was pregnant again when we married in October 1977. We weren't worried about it, because we had decided to have a baby as soon as possible, as a companion for Joanne. Strangely, I didn't feel any guilt or any conflict with my faith about this pregnancy, because somehow I knew this love was real and would last for ever. We had a beautiful wedding with my wonderful dad giving me away. I remember my dad telling me how lovely I looked. I had a beautiful long white dress and veil, and I felt so pleased walking up the aisle on my father's arm, with little Joanne as bridesmaid, along with my two nieces, Karen and Suzanne, and Barry's sister, Dawn. The service was beautiful. We had a full nuptial Mass even though Barry was not a Catholic, and I received the Holy Sacrament. Our honeymoon was in the New Forest, in a very beautiful hotel, so the New Forest has always been a very special place for me.

When we were first married, I was a bit of a lapsed Catholic, inasmuch as I didn't go to Mass every week. I did feel guilty about it, as my early religious instruction had taught me that we must go every Sunday, and my confession was very rare at the time, but I must say that I always felt the strength of God's love and His presence with me at all times. When the children started school and it was necessary to start going to Mass more regularly and take part in church activities, I began to embrace the Church more myself. The more I did, the more Barry would be there at my side, supporting and encouraging me. Barry wasn't a Catholic then; he'd been baptized and confirmed in the Anglican Church, but he wasn't an active churchgoer, although he was always happy to come along with me. As time went on, though, he became more and *more interested in Catholicism, until eventually he made the decision to convert to the faith. He took on the faith with a passion, twenty-two years ago. He seemed not to be able to get enough of it. He has since thoroughly embraced it, pursuing it with tremendous enthusiasm, through reading, researching, regular churchgoing, retreats, Bible study, prayer – his love for God is overwhelming. He does very little without praying about it first.*

*Danny was born in 1978, then Billy in 1980, and then in 1982, just after we'd moved from our first home in Mottingham to Lee, Tommy was born. So we had Joanne and three lovely little boys, all very placid, happy, well-behaved children. Barry worked very hard, seven days a week, and I was working with him in the car spares shops as much as I could. I was pregnant again very quickly with Bobby, another lovely little boy. Life wasn't without its ups and downs: Tommy had whooping cough and then asthma as a baby, and poor Bobby was also very unwell and was constantly in and out of hospital with bronchiolitis. Eventually he was taken into the Brompton Hospital for tests. The tests showed he had an immune deficiency, so the whole family was tested, and it turned out that Barry and I both had something in our blood that was causing the deficiency. But Bobby was such a good baby:we'd take him into the Brompton Hospital and leave him overnight, then go back the next morning. He would have slept all night and not even known we'd been away!*

. . . . . . . . . . . . .

*Samantha was born in 1986. It was a normal pregnancy, and she was born about nine in the evening. We were so pleased to have another girl, after a run of four boys, although I do remember thinking when she was born that she wasn't very pretty. I phoned my sister the next morning, all excited to have had a little girl, and I said, "She's not very pretty, but she's so lovely."*

*The next thing I remember is all these doctors standing round my bed saying, "Mummy, now I think you know what we're going to tell you." I honestly didn't have a clue. "Your baby has Down's syndrome." It was devastating. My view of Down's syndrome was the negative stereotype – fat people with pudding-basin haircuts and so on – and there was a centre in Lewisham for people with disabilities where you'd see them all coming out. I held Samantha, scared and praying so hardto Our Lady. Our next-door neighbour Kathleen, who was a dear friend, came to visit me in hospital and* said, in her broad Irish accent, "Oh, the poor little darlin'!" and gave me some rosary beads, which gave me some comfort.

I took Sam home and just wanted to get her into church, to protect her, thinking she'd be safe if I could get her there. It's very strange, looking back, how it affected me. I couldn't do that at first because she was what they called "failing to thrive". She wasn't putting on weight, so she was back in hospital after ten days. I remember pouring holy water on her. Looking back, I ask myself what was the matter with me, what did I think that would achieve? I think I was scared. I didn't know what the future held for her. I knew I'd never let her go, and I'd love her with all my heart, but if I'm honest, it was very scary.

It never turned out to be the scary thing that I thought it would be. She was beautiful; she had long ginger hair, the same colour as the boys' hair when they were born, and she was the most contented, happy baby. The special needs health visitor, Louise, came round to visit us. She sat down and said, "Before we talk about anything, you have the option to give up your baby." It was very common then, but we wouldn't think of it; absolutely never would we ever give her up. We knew that we'd love Samantha, and she's turned out to be a joy. Louise was a great support to us.

It was very important to me that she should become part of God's family, so we had Sam baptized very quickly too. We had a bit of a party after the baptism, and there were lots of people round at our house that afternoon. At one point I couldn't find Barry. I eventually found him sitting on the bedroom floor, next to Sam's cot, crying. I suppose that was when our thinking started to change.

We knew nothing of people with disabilities, although I would honestly say that we are by nature caring and compassionate people. Here we were, faced with the situation first-hand. We launched ourselves into the challenge head first: we sought to meet other families with Down's syndrome children, we started up the Lewisham Down's Group, and our every waking moment was to do with Down's syndrome – trying to work out ways to make life better for our baby.

I hope and pray that my other children don't feel that they missed out. We always included them in everything we were doing, but we have never discussed it very much from their point of view. They have always just gone along with *whatever we have done as parents, with no complaints. It was, indeed, a big jolt to our family at the time, and the other children had to accustom themselves to the big change that came over the family, but they seemed to meet everything with courage and compassion. We couldn't have asked for more understanding and support from them than they have given over the years. We still all support each other endlessly, and arguments and unkind words are rare in my house.*

*Sam's education has always been very difficult. When she was three, she went to a special school, where the teachers were absolutely delightful. But the feeling in those days was that children with disabilities should go on to mainstream schools. We were going to church every week as a family by this time, prompted maybe by the crisis of having a child with Down's syndrome, and had moved our children to the school attached to our parish church. So we started Sam in the Infants at St Winifred's, and on the whole it went well. When she was ready to go up to the Juniors, we wanted her to go full-time. Although of course Sam was academically way behind every other child, we felt that the school could cope and meet her needs. She could talk a little, in a very basic fashion, so we applied to the school for her to go full-time, but were turned down. We felt terribly hurt by it, particularly because the school governors were mostly friends from church. We decided to go to an appeal tribunal, which was very hard, standing in dispute with the head teacher, who was a lovely person. But she couldn't convince the tribunal that Sam wouldn't be able to cope, and Lewisham Education Authority didn't put a very good case either, so we won the appeal.*

*Sam went full-time into the Juniors, and part of me feels it was the worst thing I've ever done. Unfortunate things happened: she went on a school journey, and one of the Learning Support Assistants trimmed her fringe. I was very angry; what right had they to do this? They wouldn't have done it to another child. The day before she left the primary school, she had to take in a white shirt to be signed and also a contact book, but nothing was written on either of them, and I was terribly hurt for her; I felt she had been neglected. Next, we were "lucky enough", as we thought, to get her into a mainstream Catholic secondary school, where we knew a lot of people, but that didn't work either. I believe with all my heart it could have worked, but their view was simply that Sam was "the least able child we've ever had". They asked us if we'd considered boarding school.*

*One day one of my sons came home from school and said, "Mum, I saw some boys flicking elastic bands at Sam." It turned out to be a young boy we knew very well. We went to the school and they said they would talk to the boy in question. We said, "Don't just talk to the boy – talk to the parents as well! This is unacceptable behaviour." Then Samantha received a letter of apology from the boy, but this little incident, along with other episodes of bullying, knocked her confidence badly at secondary school.*

*I still believe mainstream education is the right option for a child with Down's, and that any child will thrive in a mainstream school if they're wanted. But if a child is not wanted, they won't thrive, and that's what I felt happened. So we put her into a full-time special school, but by that time her confidence had gone. She doesn't talk very much now. I'm not blaming either of the schools; I take full responsibility. All my children went through that secondary school, and I've got a really good relationship with all the staff past and present, so I blame no one but myself for things not working. I feel I missed something somewhere along the line. In hindsight, I feel she should probably have gone to a special school, where they could have dealt with her needs. But all our friends with Down's syndrome children were putting them into mainstream education. This was the received wisdom at the time, and we felt we should go with the flow. Maybe it was a mistake; maybe she would or could have done better. We will never know.*

．．．．．．．．．．．．

*In the meantime, Joanne had become pregnant aged fifteen and had a baby at sixteen. We didn't find out she was pregnant till very early January 1988. She was seven months pregnant and one of her friends phoned us. It was a terrific shock at the time, because she was so young. Her baby boy, James, was born two months later. His father was Michael, Joanne's best friend's brother, and he was only seventeen. Their relationship didn't last very long, and because of it there were some bad feelings between the two families at the time. This resulted in a difficult and upsetting period of dispute over James's custody.*

*Eventually, after what seemed to be a much longer time than it actually was, Joanne was awarded custody and she and James lived with us. We often waste energy and heartache in pointless disputes, involving lawyers when we would be much better sorting things out informally and probably coming to the* same outcome in the end. Joanne did meet and fall in love with another young man eventually, Tony, and they married when she was aged nearly eighteen. They moved into a flat together with James and seemed happy together for a while, but it was a very volatile relationshipwhich lasted two or three years, and to be honest I was surprised it lasted as long as it did.

James loved being at our house and playing with our children, who were, of course, his uncles and aunt, and when he eventually started at primary school with our boys, he always wanted to come home with me after school. He sometimes stayed with us at weekends and he was a very lively lad, quite different from our boys, who were always very quiet and laid back, so we always knew he was around! When Joanne's marriage broke up, James was aged five.

Following the break-up of her marriage, Joanne began to develop mental health problems, which became very severe. At the beginning of August 1993 we were going on our first ever holiday abroad, to France. We took James with us, but Joanne stayed at home because she was so unwell and very badly depressed. My sister took care of her for the three weeks and she recalls now that although they had been very close, always, it was like living with a stranger for those three weeks.

In early October that year, Joanne suddenly became very unwell overnight: she became delusional, she was hearing voices, she thought she was dying – it was horrendous and terribly frightening. She was walking around the house with a duvet over her head, and the doctors kept saying, "Take your medication," but she refused because she was terrified that we were trying to kill her. Eventually the doctor, the social worker, and the psychiatrist came and said, "You take your medication now, or you'll have to go into hospital." She still refused, and my beloved daughter was sectioned and sent to Bexley Hospital.

It was a dreadful, old-fashioned, frightening, horror-story ofa place where she was forced to take medication and locked in. We were all at our wits' end. She was sectioned for twenty-eight days. I had no idea how grim the hospital would be. I had this vision in my mind that it would be painted yellow– I don't know why I thought that – and that she was going to get the best care possible. Six people had to hold her down to inject the drugs into her. I remember praying and praying to God, it was so awful. It was the most terrible time for poor Joanne. I often think how scared she must have been. It was very hard for us, too, trying to care for someone with a mental illness, as well as look after little James and all the other children.

James has never really left us since then, although eventually, slowly, Joanne's mental illness began to show signs of improvement. James has always had a warm relationship with his mum, and of course Joanne wanted him to come back to live with her, but he found it hard to extricate himself from our large family home with its fun and bustle. My children are like his brothers and sisters and I know that's how they see him. He's now in his twenties and has a great relationship with his mum. They adore each other, but he still lives at my house. He has a good relationship with his dad also and sees him regularly. Michael went on to become an IT academic and is married with four other children. Looking back, there have been some difficult times between us, but life is far too short to hold grudges, and I have great respect for his grandparents on his father's side and for Michael now. They were all a great support to James and indeed to us after Jimmy's death, and old wounds were very much healed.

Joanne still struggles at times with her mental illness. She has good and bad days, but thankfully she has never regressed to the intensity of how it was at the beginning. She understands it more now herself and knows how important it is to take her medication. It has been very hard for her, since Jimmy's death. He was her dearest friend as well as her brother. Sometimes she cries and cries. I worry about her and sometimes feel helpless as a mother. People have often said to me, "Oh, having a child with Down's syndrome — how difficult for you." Not at all! But having someone with mental health problems — oh my goodness me! Apart from losing our Jimmy, it has been the hardest thing in my life, to see my beautiful, kind, sweet, beloved daughter suffer as she has.

Allthrough these difficult times I have prayed for God's strength and guidance. Our challenges with Samantha's and Joanne's problems actually made my faith grow even stronger. I really feel God's loving arms around me when times are so hard. On one occasion, I was trying to sort out some housing issues for Joanne and I was having a really difficult day, and at one point I was all alone and just fell to my knees. I can see myself doing it now, falling to my knees and praying to Our Lady, because I felt I couldn't go on much longer. And I felt this strange and powerful sensation of being lifted up, and I knew then that I could go on.

*Joanne is a kind and generous person with a wonderful nature and, in the face of all adversity, has taken to helping out in our coffee shop as a volunteer from time to time. More importantly, she has taken on voluntary work for others with mental illness, taking people out who may be unable to travel by themselves or afraid to go out, or who don't have the confidence to go to the doctor's or a hospital or shopping on their own. She excels at this, despite all the difficulties she has struggled with every step of the way. These people trust her implicitly and she does her best never to let them down. She does amazing work, and we are so proud of her. My heart aches for her, but we try always to be positive. I constantly pray to God that He will make her better.*

# 4

# Jimmy

*Our next child, Harry, was born in 1989, a big baby and a real mummy's boy; when he was a baby he wouldn't go to anyone but me. He was a beautiful, dark-haired boy and is now the gentlest, kindest young man you could hope to meet. I'd had an amniocentesis when I was pregnant with Harry. I really don't know why. I suppose, after Sam, I wanted to know whether the baby would have a problem, but afterwards I thought, "Why did I do that?" Sam was so good, I felt it wouldn't have mattered if the next baby had had Down's. Maybe I wanted to prepare myself.*

*I certainly didn't think about it with Jimmy, or George, because I always said if all my babies had been like Samantha, life would be so easy! At bedtime, she'd go to bed without any complaints; she'd get up in the morning, she'd giggle and laugh and was never naughty. Sam has always been the most delightful person, with no behavioural problems at all. She loves me and absolutely hates me being upset. If she sees me crying (which is not very often) it worries her. She'll cry, "Mummy, mummy, mummy…" She does have problems with her speech. For some reason she has regressed as far as that is concerned, but she signs and she says a few words and we all get by. We have lots of laughs.*

. . . . . . . . . . . . .

*Jimmy was conceived when we were on holiday in Norfolk and born on Cup Final Day, Saturday 9 May 1992. He was a week late, and then, on the Friday, Joanne was helping me out at home. She gave me a cup of raspberry leaf tea, which is supposed to induce labour, but nothing happened. The next morning, she gave me another cup. My dad phoned at noon and asked, "Anything happened yet, Marn?" "No, Dad, nothing yet."*

*The next thing I knew, by one o'clock, I was phoning Barry to come home from work. We got to the hospital at two, and by half past two, Jimmy was born! It was as quick as that, and Barry got home for the second half of the Cup Final. We've always laughed about that. Jimmy was the most beautiful baby, 10 pounds 4 ounces, the easiest birth, and I brought him home the next day. James was away that weekend, so when he came back home, there was a new baby waiting for him, and he asked if he could name him Jimmy. There was a lot of excitement and delight in the house that weekend.*

*At four months, Jimmy got meningitis. I can remember that day very clearly: Jimmy had been unwell the week before. I'd called the doctor, who'd prescribed some medicine, and Jimmy seemed fine. This particular morning he woke up, and I brought him downstairs and said to Barry, "Jimmy doesn't seem very well – he looks a really odd colour." He'd gone rather grey. So once Barry had taken the older children to school – I still had three small children at home at that point – I phoned the doctor's and got a mid-morning appointment. I thought I'd do some housework in the meantime, so I went up to the boys' bedroom. There were videos all over the floor, and as I was climbing up to put them away, the cupboard I was standing on gave way, and my feet went through the top. My legs were bleeding and I couldn't find any trousers to wear, so I put a pair of the boys' tracksuit trousers on and went back downstairs. Jimmy was foaming at the mouth. Trying not to panic, I phoned the doctor's and they said, "Come straight away."*

*I rushed down there, carrying Jimmy, with all the little ones running behind me, and my GP, Dr Bentham, was absolutely wonderful. He's Catholic as well, and every time I had a baby, he and his wife seemed to be having a baby too – they have thirteen now! As soon as he examined Jimmy, he said, "You need to get him to hospital." So I drove straight to the hospital, running through the car park again with all these children scampering along behind me, and rushed in with Jimmy. They did a lumbar puncture and said, "He's got meningitis."*

*It was very frightening. I'd had lots of scares with Bobby, but when Jimmy was diagnosed with meningitis, it was like my worst nightmare coming true. Many things have happened in my life, which previously I'd thought would be my worst nightmare, but somehow we've managed to live through them. There have been many times when I've thought, "It can't get worse than this," only to be proved wrong later: having a child with Down's syndrome, having a pregnant teenage daughter, having a child with meningitis, having a child* with a mental illness, discovering one of your children is gay – these were all things I dreaded before they happened to me, but God has given us the strength to cope with all these things.

Jimmy had what they call haemophilus meningitis and he was in hospital for two weeks. The hospital staff were absolutely brilliant. I had to stay there with Jimmy, and sleep overnight. Friends and family rallied round to look after all our other children while Barry was at work. We were very worried that the illness might damage Jimmy's mental development, but nothing was affected. He had a special test at Guy's Hospital, where they put babies to sleep and check their response to sound waves, and he was fine.

Right from the start, everything about Jimmy was different. Even when he was just a few weeks old, I remember worrying and going to the doctor's, because he was so easy! He was an unusually good baby, and grew quickly into a lovely little boy. He was always smiling. He had a beautiful smile. There was an innocence and a boldness about him, and an uncomplicated love of life.

Nothing ever really got Jimmy down. I don't remember him ever being upset about anything and I don't ever remember telling him off. The worst I remember is maybe telling him to put his washing in the dirty basket. All my children were calm and laid back, but Barry and I would often say, "There's something different about Jimmy." I think it was his happy, carefree nature, not worrying about things, wanting to join in with everything that was going on. He never minded staying away from home. He'd be down at my mum's and my sister's quite a lot, and he'd help them, at a young age. Even when he was tiny, he used to go over to my friend Eileen's house, just opposite us, every Saturday, and he'd watch Casualty with her and have fish for his tea. All my kids hated fish, but not Jimmy! He always had more experimental tastes in food, like putting tabasco on his scrambled eggs when he was a toddler, or tuna and sardine sandwiches for his packed lunches. My other kids would pull faces and say, "Yuk!"

When Jimmy went to nursery, they spotted that he had a language disorder – not a speech impediment, but a problem with not taking in what was being said to him, so he was assessed at St Thomas' Hospital and it turned out that his behaviour was "absolutely perfect" but that he was struggling in certain areas.

Then, from the moment Jimmy got to school, he struggled with schoolwork. When he was about seven, since the school was saying he was too young to have a statement of special needs, we got a private educational psychologist from the Dyslexia Association to test Jimmy. The results showed that he was very dyslexic, but had a high level of common sense. It was lovely to see him take those tests: from the point of view of behaviour, he sailed through. Nothing fazed him; he'd try anything.

Jimmy never worried about the fact that he was struggling; it never bothered him. He needed extra support in school – so what? All the teachers loved him and wanted him in their class. The Special Educational Needs Coordinator really liked him; she even used to bring him cups of tea! He had masses of friends. His nature was just delightful. I never remember Jimmy being grumpy; the only tantrum I can ever remember him having was when he was about two years old, on a family holiday to Dymchurch. We'd gone to a little funfair, and it was time to leave and Jimmy was jumping up and down, screaming, "I don't wanna go!" We've got a bit of camcorder footage of that; Jimmy used to cringe when we showed it. His classroom assistant Sarah, who was known for having a choice way with words, once said of Jimmy, "Not a brat bone in his body."

If anything needed to be done at home, he would do it, from a young age. He was very good at mending things and painting things. He'd fix a broken chair for me and revarnish it, or go round to our elderly next-door neighbour, Kathleen, and cut her grass for her and have a chat, and she'd always offer him money, and he'd always refuse it.

His interests tended to skip from one thing to another. Danny plays rugby for Sidcup, so Jimmy growing up wanted to play as well. Of course he wanted all the gear, the boots and everything, and then he'd lose interest! It was the same with fishing: we'd got him the rod and the fishing tackle, but you couldn't get him to stick with one thing. He used to have a laugh going fishing with Joanne's boyfriend, Andy. On one trip, Jimmy sat on a box of maggots in the car and they went everywhere, and within a couple of days Joanne's car was full of great big bluebottles!

He had an impulsive nature, a happy-go-lucky quality, ambling along and taking an interest in just about everything he came across, but it could be frustrating sometimes. You'd be sitting in the kitchen talking about something,

*and Jimmy would come in and join in the conversation halfway through –*
*"What's all that about, then?" and then divert it somewhere else. The next*
*minute you'd be saying, "Oh, Jim! I've completely lost my train of thought!"*

*He could talk to anybody. As he got older, he could talk to children; he'd be so*
*kind to them. We have a friend of the family who took many, many years to have*
*a baby, and Jimmy must have been about six or seven when their son was born.*
*Jimmy used to go round there and play with him. He'd play with William all*
*the time, because he knew how to be with young children. But he knew how to be*
*with adults as well. A letter we received from a local resident after Jimmy died*
*gave us a lovely picture of how people in our neighbourhood saw him:*

> Dear Mr & Mrs Mizen,
>
> My name is Karen. I live opposite the Citroen car
> showroom. I just wanted to say to you both, I am with
> and thinking of you. Your son was so helpful to me; if I
> asked he would help me carry my shopping from the car
> to my home, when I could not manage or was in pain.
> Your son Jimmy had an old head on young shoulders:
> kind, caring, helpful, and polite. I am really going to
> miss his shy smile, when I am in the garden. May God
> guide and protect, bless, and keep you all strong.
>
> God bless – Karen

*He had a great confidence in social situations. My children love bread, and*
*if we were in a restaurant, they'd always want more and more bread rolls,*
*poppadoms, whatever was on offer. We'd say, "Jimmy, go and sort it out for*
*us," and he wouldn't mind doing it, whereas the others would be embarrassed.*
*Nothing embarrassed Jimmy.*

*He was a great diplomat, a peacemaker, but he also knew right from*
*wrong and he used to stand up for his friends at school. It got him into a few*
*sticky situations; I remember him being told off at school because he wouldn't*
*"grass" on a boy. If someone was being horrible to a friend, he would try*
*to sort it out, in the right way. On one occasion, when a boy at school had*

*been excluded for the day, Jimmy came home and said to Barry, who was a governor at the school, "Dad, that boy's innocent. You have to go and sort it out." He had a kind of authority that came with his size – he was always so much bigger than his friends, it was quite comical to see them going out, because they only came up to his waist! His friends' parents used to say, "Oh, if Jimmy Mizen's going, you'll be all right. You're in good company."*

*Jimmy would be the one to sort out disputes; he'd stand between the people quarrelling and say, "Come on, let's sort this out." I don't ever remember Jimmy being in a fight at school. If there was ever any trouble at home, say if George was having trouble with the young boys next door, we'd get Jimmy to go and sort it out. As Barry says, he had a boldness that was endearing.*

*He had a special friendship with each of his siblings and with his nephew James. With Danny, it was based around rugby – they used to call Jimmy "little Dan" at the rugby club. With Tommy, it was music: teaching Jim a bit of guitar, sharing CD collections, and so on. He was almost like a best friend to Joanne. She could really open up to him. When he was doing his work experience at Leathermarket JMB, she'd get messages from him through the day, saying how it was going. We found out after Jimmy died that he used to enjoy having the odd cigarette with James.*

*I don't know whether Jimmy ever really had a girlfriend. There were a couple of girls who were particularly upset after he died, both thinking they were his girlfriend, and a few weeks before, he'd met a girl called Georgia at the rugby club and then arranged to meet her the day he was killed. She wrote to us afterwards:*

> For the short amount of time I knew Jimmy, it seemed like I had known him for ever. We got on really well, we kept in touch through texting and speaking on MSN to each other. We told each other everything. On the day Jimmy died, we had arranged to meet up at the rugby club that afternoon to celebrate his birthday. Although I had seen Jimmy at the club before, we never spoke, until one Saturday, when I was sitting with a few of my friends, when Jimmy came over and said, "Excuse me love, is anyone sitting here?" He sat down and started

chatting to us. He had us all in fits of laughter. We were
all sitting on the field under the rugby posts, when I
found a pair of children's pink sunglasses. I showed
them to Jimmy and he laughed and said, "Arr George,
put them on me and take a photo," so I put them on
him and Charlotte Murphy took the picture.

*The school had arranged some counselling for the pupils after Jimmy's
death, and these three girls were devastated, so the counsellor suggested they
should make something for Jimmy and give it to us. Georgia and two of her
school friends made the most beautiful memorial plaque for Jimmy – out of
jelly beans.*

*The girl I think Jimmy really liked was a friend's daughter; they were
born about the same time and had grown up together. I don't know what the
full story was, but I think she's been struggling ever since he died.*

. . . . . . . . . . . . .

*Barry had sold the car spares business in 1984, because he wanted to spend
more time with his family and go to church on Sundays instead of working.
He was getting a faith by this time; when he was in his late thirties, he did the
"Journey of Faith" course at our church, and since then it's played the biggest
part in his life. Just going to church on a Sunday wasn't enough. We had a
great spiritual thirst, so we joined an ecumenical community called "Couples
for Christ", which met for Bible study and prayer and worship. The first
time we went to the main meeting of the community, they were laying hands
on people and praying for them, and they were all falling down. I thought,
"That's not going to happen to me!" and I sat down on a chair. I've never
fallen down like that and I'm never sure whether people are just doing it on
purpose or whether it's the Holy Spirit, but it was certainly never going to
happen to me. I was very nervous of the Bible study, which was very alien
to me, but I loved the prayer and praise. The first time I really learned and
remembered a passage from the Bible was when Joanne became ill, and Barry
read this to me: "Come to me, all who are weary and heavy-laden, and I will
give you rest" (Matthew 11:28). But being a member of a community wasnot
always easy; it was a real eye-opener.*

*Barry sold the shop and decided to take some time off work. He'd been working non-stop seven days a week for more than ten years, and he wanted to take some time out to think about what to do next. The business had been profitable; it didn't bring in a huge fortune, but it was enough to pay a mortgage and put food on the table. The sale gave us enough money to last for a year and not have to worry, and still have enough to buy another business at the end of it to make a living.*

*We bought the shoe repair shop in 1985. Barry had never repaired a shoe in his life, but he learned all the skills very quickly. He's very able in that way: he picks things up very fast. Anything he turns his hand to, he does well: not only is he very academic, he's also very good with his hands. We knew the shop probably wouldn't produce enough income for us on its own, and we'd have to run another business alongside it, so after we'd had the shoe repair shop for a year we bought a grocery store. We called it Marn Foods! It turned out to be one of our worst moves, because the day we completed the purchase, Samantha was born. Rather than worrying about this new business, we had a daughter with Down's syndrome to think about. Also, the following April, a big Sainsbury's opened up in the area. Running the grocer's and making a profit became very hard work. I workedthere with all my children coming in with me. We did havesome staff, but I had to be there most of the time. We'd sold a shop because we didn't want to work seven days a week, and here we were now working seven days a week once again, so after three years we sold it. It was one of the hardest jobs we ever had together and, with everything else that was going on in our lives, with Samantha and Joanne, life seemed very tough. But we coped, we laughed, and as a family we stayed solid.*

. . . . . . . . . . . . .

*Even when they were very young, Jimmy and Harry used to go to work with Barry. I can see them now: they'd have their little white aprons on, and both of them would have their little box of tools and their little bottle of water – water, not glue – and be pasting the bottoms of the shoes and not understanding why these shoes weren't sticking together. Because Daddy used glue, they thought it was glue! They looked so sweet in the window, and people used to pass the shop and go, "Ah!" They were never naughty in the shop. They wouldn't mess up, or misbehave, or spill things; they'd just think they were helping.*

*Jimmy became Barry's little partner, his Saturday boy, and as time went on, he learned to work there properly. They'd go off in the morning, and they'd be whistling together and having a giggle about something, or singing a song. That's all gone from Barry now. I can see it gone from his eyes. I can see the pain there, of missing his son, his friend. Barry has a special relationship with each of our children – Harry was his football partner, and with Danny it's rugby, but with Jimmy it was a happy-go-lucky, dad and son off to work together relationship. There was no hidden agenda with Jimmy; what you saw was absolutely what you got. It's a busy little shop, and Jimmy was a big lad, and sometimes he wouldn't wait to be asked. He'd just say, "Oh, I'll do that, Dad!" and shove himself right in there and get in Barry's way. Barry would say, "Jimmy, just stand over there a minute and let me get on and do the work!" Jimmy was so keen to get stuck in, and very talented with his hands; Barry was impressed with how quickly he picked things up. He liked using the till, and serving the customers, and taking the money – they all liked that! Barry would pay him, at the end of the day, and sometimes, if Jimmy had been late that morning, he'd say, "That's too much, Dad," and give some back.*

*Jimmy had done a work experience placement the year before he died, through a friend of my sister, who had managed to set him up for a couple of weeks with a property maintenance company in Southwark: Leathermarket JMB. He'd said to Barry, "Dad, whatever I do, I have to go there on a train, otherwise it isn't proper work." The placement was at London Bridge, and he enjoyed travelling with the other commuters. It involved him going out each day with a fitter, repairing doors and bathrooms and so on. By all accounts this man who was the fitter was pretty sullen and resentful at having a "kid" foisted on him, as he saw it, but by the end of the fortnight, Jimmy had bowled him over, and they were the best of friends. After this work experience, Leathermarket JMB decided to create an apprenticeship for him! This was the job he would have gone to after his GCSEs, and after he died, they sent us this wonderful letter:*

Dear Barry,

Jimmy came to the JMB on work experience in 2007. He showed great potential as a repairs operative. His enthusiasm to learn was infectious and he quickly became part of the team. His ability to work with residents was excellent. Leathermarket JMB is in a very diverse area and he was able to relate to everyone he met regardless of their age, ethnic background, or circumstances. This is a rare ability, especially in someone so young.

Leathermarket JMB's experience with Jimmy opened our eyes to the potential of bringing young people into the company and training them up. As a direct result of Jimmy working with us, Ron Elston, our Repairs Manager, worked with our directors to set up a new apprentice scheme – something we had never undertaken before. We agreed a partnership with Lewisham College for two Leathermarket JMB apprentices on their NVQ programme.

Ron Elston remained in contact with Jimmy after he went back to school and was very keen that Jimmy joined our new apprentice scheme. Jimmy's influence continues, as we want to launch the apprentice scheme this summer in his memory. We would be really honoured to name the scheme after Jimmy as a positive legacy of the potential that Jimmy had. Ron said that you are interested in us doing this and may want to get involved. This would be very welcome.

We were all greatly saddened by the loss of Jimmy, but really want to do something positive as thanks to Jimmy for opening our eyes to the potential of young people.

Yours sincerely,
Andy Bates
Leathermarket JMB Manager

*To think that our son made such an impact in just two weeks, in what is quite a tough, hard-working environment, has made us very, very proud.*

. . . . . . . . . . . .

*It's difficult to know, but I felt that Jimmy had a strong faith. Often, when Barry and I were sitting down in the mornings and doing our daily Bible readings, Jimmy would come and sit with us. We'd say, "Let's say our prayer for the day, Jim," and he'd join in. We'd go to church on a Sunday, and sometimes I couldn't get him out of bed, but the next thing I knew, he'd be there at the back, and as he went up to communion, he'd look down at us with that big, beautiful smile. We never put any pressure on him or any of the children to come to church, especially as they became teenagers, but Jimmy liked coming along. He seemed to have a good grasp of the values of our faith; he got an A for his GCSE in Religious Education, based on his coursework. He wrote about Martin Luther King and racial equality, and about gender discrimination, and in one answer, about the Parable of the Good Samaritan, he wrote, "Everyone is your neighbour. You don't need to like them, just respect them." Then, later, ironically, he wrote, "Jesus told us, Thou shalt not murder, but people still do it."*

*We used to go to the New Dawn Conference, a charismatic Catholic festival held at Walsingham every year. Jimmy loved it so much, putting up the tents and helping cook breakfast for all the campers. He looked forward to it every year. He didn't go off to the Youth Camp; he was much more comfortable with the adults and would stay with our little group of friends, where we were camped. When we all went to Mass each day, all the kids would come along too. We never said they had to come; they just wanted to and they were happy to join in. You can go to an outdoor reconciliation (or confession) at New Dawn; it's in a big field, with lots of priests stationed all around, and we would queue up. All of a sudden Jimmy would join us, not because we'd said, "You must go to reconciliation," but from his own choice. We have always believed, with the children, that once they get to a certain age, if it's going to mean anything to them, going to church has got to be their choice. There's no point in forcing them.*

*Sometimes, I'd be sitting at the shrine to Our Lady of Walsingham, just contemplating, and Jimmy would come along and sit down next to me. Harry would do that sometimes as well. I feel Jimmy had a special faith, and this was God working in preparation for what was going to happen.*

. . . . . . . . . . . . .

*About two years after Jimmy was born, I had a very distressing miscarriage. I was the mother of all these beautiful children – how could I be losing a baby? I had a very difficult time at the hospital. They sent me for a scan, and there were all these other mothers, and I was in a wheelchair, bleeding heavily and losing my precious baby. It was at thirteen weeks, but it felt like a long way on to me. I hadn't actually told anyone I was pregnant; it wasn't because I wanted to keep it a secret, but maybe I was afraid of what other people's reactions might be – "Oh goodness, not another baby…" I grieved terribly after it, then not long afterwards I had another miscarriage. For some reason it didn't cause me the grief I felt with the first miscarriage, but it was still very distressing. I was about forty-three then. A couple of years later we were on holiday in Wales, and Barry and I walked around the beach together, praying for another baby. George was conceived on that holiday.*

*He was another big baby, over 10 pounds. George was a bonny baby and he has grown into a wonderful boy with a gorgeous nature. We have always thought of him as a gift from God. There's nothing angry or violent about George. Everyone adores him – my sister, my friend Eileen, Joanne – and he's the most precious boy, full of love and kindness. He struggles at school, much like Jimmy, with a language disorder and dyslexia, but he doesn't mind having a statement and likes his Learning Support Assistants. But I do worry about George: he has an awful lot of pressure on him. Our life now is very much about Jimmy: everything we do is to do with Jimmy, and Barry and I also go away more than we've ever done before. I do hope it doesn't affect George too much. For three years after Jimmy's death, he slept on our bedroom floor, and was always very careful to make sure the windows were closed and the curtains drawn with no gaps and the door shut. He couldn't face sleeping in the bedroom he'd shared with Jimmy. He's got a few friends at school, but mostly loves being at home and around his family. Danny and his partner Fay have recently had a baby daughter, Eva, and George dotes on her. George is a real character and everyone's joy, but since Jimmy's death everyone's clung to George, and I think it's a big weight for him. He has a great faith: he's an altar server at church, and he'll often sit down with me and say some prayers. He's always the one to say grace at mealtimes.*

. . . . . . . . . . . .

*My mum had a stroke in June 2003, which was devastating for the family.*
*She was unable to eat, walk, or talk. She was the matriarch of the family and*
*kept us all in order, but she was the kindest, loveliest of mothers, and all our*
*friends were drawn to her and adored her. At parties she would "hold court"*
*and we used to call her "Good Queen Bess" (Bess being her name). It was*
*very comforting, just being in her presence. After the stroke she was in hospital*
*for about three months; they did their best, but it became clear that there wasn't*
*much more they could do for her, so we had to make a decision about her future.*
*She lived with my sister up until her illness, but as my sister worked full-time,*
*the decision was made that Mum would come to my home and I would look*
*after her. I had to learn to look after her properly, as she had to be fed through*
*a tube in her stomach. I was worried about whether I would be able to provide*
*such a high level of care, but I managed.*

*The house became a hive of activity, with carers coming back and forth*
*constantly and my brother and sister visiting her regularly. I had to learn how*
*to give her medication, through her drip-feed. But undoubtedly it was the right*
*decision; it was a strangely wonderful time in our lives. It was just such a*
*pleasure having Mum around, in her wheelchair, still laughing and joking as*
*best she could, and the house felt a vibrant place, always buzzing with visitors.*
*The most important thing in Mum's life was her family. We never, at any time,*
*considered a residential care home for her. I was determined to learn how to*
*administer the drip-feed and the medication, and we managed. As tragic as this*
*time was for Mum and for all of us, I have to say that those months when she*
*had all of us around her, both in the hospital and at home, were happy months,*
*in their own way, because we all loved her so much and she loved us. She used*
*to laugh, still, even though she couldn't talk very much. Looking back, it was a*
*wonderful time in our lives. Mum was such a lovely person to have around, and*
*caring for her turned out to be a joy for me and the rest of the family.*

*The night before she died, it was clear that she wasn't going to last much*
*longer. We were all round her bed; George was singing, "Twinkle, twinkle,*
*little star." She died, we wept, and we sang. We had a beautiful funeral which*
*really celebrated her life and was sad but joyful.*

*After Jimmy died, I so longed to have my mum's arms around me, and I*
*missed her and my dad more than anything. I used to imagine my dad phoning*
*me up and telling me everything would be OK. But I did feel they were with*

*me, with their love and support – it's difficult to describe, but they were making me strong, strong enough to face the tragedy and the ordeal that had befallen us, and I was comforted.*

. . . . . . . . . . . . .

*Barry and I have had a lot of complications and challenges in our lives, but these have just drawn us closer together. I think we've had a very strong relationship from day one. We've always been able to talk things through. Some people would say that God was testing us, but I don't believe that God really ever tests us. Others would say that He heaps onto people certain things that He feels they can cope with. I have been able to cope, and come out of it quite strong, I think. But there have been times when I don't always want to cope. I sometimes think, "Why do I have to cope with something else?"*

*I was reflecting the other day, "What gift, what talents, has God given me?" I think He's given me a gift for love and care. He certainly hasn't given me a musical voice or an academic life. But I think He has given me a voice, and the courage to speak. Sometimes, with all the amazing things Barry comes out with, I think I've nothing to say in comparison. I can only speak with my heart. But I've had to find a voice. When Joanne started at primary school, the year Barry and I got married, it was coming up to the Queen's Silver Jubilee, so the head teacher wanted people to come and help prepare for a Jubilee Party. I fancied helping out with that, so I got involved, and from then on, it became a Parent-Teacher Association. I joined and eventually became chair of the PTA at the children's primary school. Then I joined the PTA at Samantha's school and I became chair of that as well*

*I had to have a voice! Even though my knees would knock together, and I'd think, "How on earth am I going to do all the introductions and summing up and so on at the AGMs? I'm going to have to do it!", I'd get Barry to help me write whatever I needed to say, and then I'd read it, and I think that's how I started to find my voice. On one occasion, at the special school, we were trying to raise a lot of money for some special playground equipment, and we raised something like seventy or eighty thousand pounds, so I became a bit of a spokesperson for that project. It's almost as if God was leading me or teaching me to be able to speak in public, because prior to that, I wouldn't have said boo to a goose.*

*When Jimmy died, we were given a voice that we never knew we had. All the things we said after Jimmy was killed, I wouldn't have expected to say. That's why I know it's God working in our lives – because I would have expected to say other things. I would have expected to be angry; I would have expected to be shouting and screaming. But we haven't done that. And it can only be God's good love. So, finding my voice through all these things seems to be part of the journey that I've had to travel.*

. . . . . . . . . . . . .

*The week before Jimmy died, Barry and I had gone away for a few days, down to Eastbourne, to go to the theatre and spend a couple of days together. It was a really strange time, because Barry was so melancholy. He had recently been looking at all our pictures of the children when they were younger, pondering family anecdotes and pining for the days when they were little. He said, "They're not there any more, are they?" We didn't have a particularly happy few days away, not because we weren't getting on, but because of this melancholy. When we thought about it afterwards, we wondered whether it was some kind of intuition about what was about to happen.*

*I'm absolutely sure we weren't meant to have Jimmy for longer than we had him. God was ready for him. And I think God had a plan for Jimmy from the moment he was born. I think He does for all of us. But for Jimmy, the plan He had for him has become quite evident.*

# 5

## Aftermath

A parade of shops leads up from a railway bridge on a normally busy main road in south-east London. Where there should be a steady flow of traffic to and from the South Circular, the road is deserted, cordoned off at the top and bottom of the hill by police vehicles with flashing blue lights. Where Saturday shoppers would normally be coming and going about their business, instead there are little knots of people spread across the pavements, standing or sitting in silence, some clinging to each other, some weeping. Blue and white police tape seals off the pavement in front of the last shop, the Three Cooks Bakery. Its glass doors are smashed, and between its maroon-painted window frames, people peering from beyond the cordon can see shattered glass strewn across the floor, a mess of spilt food, and almost everywhere, blood. Blood sprayed across the walls, smeared in a trail along the floor, blood daubed over broken glass. The bright, early May sunshine seems to have got it wrong; the sky should be grey and cold, or pouring rain. The only sounds to break the eerie silence are the occasional crackles of police walkie-talkies. Even those who are weeping do so silently.

More people arrive every few minutes, hastening to the scene from up or down the hill, or from the residential streets the other side of the main road, then slowing their pace as they take in the silent crowds, the police tape blowing in the breeze, the ambulances, and the ruined baker's shop.

Barry climbs out of the back of one of the ambulances where he has been comforting George. He wanders towards the kerb, where Tommy is sitting with his back to a tree, covered in blood, staring down at the road. His shirt and shorts and bare legs are soaked dark red with blood, his arms and hands smeared, even his neck and face. Barry sits down next to him, putting an arm round his shoulders. "All right, Tommy?" he murmurs. "I feel like I'm going to be sick," mutters Tommy.

"Barry! They've got Danny on the phone!" They both look up. Margaret is approaching, half-running, a mobile phone pressed to her ear, beckoning Barry with her other hand. "Hello? Is that Ian? Ian, it's Margaret Mizen, I need to speak to Danny, please, urgently." Standing up, her husband puts his hand on her shoulder. She clutches his sleeve. "Danny?" she cries, her mouth trembling. "Oh, Danny, Danny, Jimmy's been killed…"

· · · · · · · · · · · · ·

"I was away on a rugby tour, in Spain, with Sidcup RFC," Danny said later. "I'd woken up that morning with a huge hangover – we'd been out till 7 a.m. the night before; I went out to get some food, ended up in a bar with some friends. The next minute the chairman of the rugby club's putting me on the phone – 'Danny, it's the Lewisham Police' – and I'm thinking, 'All right, what's the laugh, what's the joke, what did I do?' Next minute he passes me the phone – it's not the police, it's my mum on the end of the phone, screaming that Jimmy's just died. I just sat in a little garden square in Valencia; I sat down for the next hour. I couldn't speak. I couldn't say a word. My little brother Jimmy wasn't around any more. I couldn't believe it was true."

· · · · · · · · · · · · ·

Now Tommy has pushed himself up from the kerb and is stumbling away, through the police tape cordon and the crowd of onlookers, who give way, gawping at his blood-soaked clothes. Several friends and neighbours pat his back as he passes; a couple ask, "Are you OK, Tommy?" but he ignores them, wandering off up the hill, his eyes pricking, his mouth set. He breathes heavily as he strides, forcing each step forwards, determined not to fall, swallowing back the gorge that rises in his throat at the smell and sticky dampness of his brother's blood all down him. *Got to get away, got to be alone, got to think, got to breathe...*

Several hundred yards up the hill, on the left, he walks into the car park of the red-brick Catholic church, Our Lady of Lourdes, where he and Jimmy and their brothers and sisters had been baptized and confirmed, where Mum and Dad went every Sunday to Mass. Where was Father Edward? He should be here at a time like this. He'd heard his mum trying to call the priest, frantically leaving messages: "Father Edward, Father Edward, where are you? I need you desperately, where are you?" No response.

He looked up at the statue of Our Lady, as if she might reach down to him, as if her expression might change. Did she know Jimmy was dead? How could she stare down unmoved, impassive at the sight of all this blood? He leaned his forehead heavily against the bricks. There were so many better ways to die. If you had to die, why not die for something, for some reason? But to choke your life out on the floor of a shop, aged sixteen, for nothing, for no reason, just a brutal waste, a beautiful young lad spilling his life-blood at the passing violent whim of some moron... *Why?* Tommy yelled, punching the wall of the church, smashing his fists into the bricks. *Why?* he cried, gasping, wincing, looking down at his skinned knuckles, bruised and trickling with fresh blood, his own blood now. He leaned for a moment, shuddering with sobs, then staggered away, blinded with tears.

· · · · · · · · · · · · ·

*You're walking around, and your whole mind is saying to yourself, what should I be doing? Should I be rolling on the floor? Should I be screaming and shouting? I wasn't doing the things that I thought I should be doing. I didn't know what to do with myself. It's just like this cloud in your head, telling you it's not happening. But you're telling yourself, "Actually, Margaret, it is. Your precious Jimmy is not going to be here any more. He's dead."*

*There were a lot of people there. I remember thinking to myself, that looks like Damien Jackson – what's Damien doing here? I didn't know why people were there. Afterwards I found out Paul, Damien's brother, had witnessed the incident. Then my sister and my brother turned up, and all my other children, and James my grandson, from different places all over London. They were all turning up, and all their friends were turning up, and neighbours, locals were turning up. I was desperate, desperate for my priest – I remember phoning him and it went onto the answer machine, and then I remembered he was away with the youth of our parish on their confirmation trip. I said to the police, "I've got to have a priest," and a priest from Lewisham turned up, Father Sean O'Connor, and I said, "Please let him in, let him go and bless my son." But they wouldn't let him in. It was a crime scene.*

· · · · · · · · · · · · ·

"So the paramedics are coming out," Barry recalls, "gloves coming off; everything else is a haze. And they're saying *he's dead*. And in a sense, I wasn't surprised. I don't know why. But my initial reaction was, *what am I supposed to do now?* Somebody says, 'OK, he's dead.' *What shall I do now?* I was baffled. I sat down on the kerb, opposite the shop. The neighbour's daughter was there, Anne; she put her hand on my shoulder and said, 'Do you want some company, or do you want to be left alone?' I said, 'Left alone.' And then you think, 'Hold on, there's George – I must do something.' I sat at the back of the ambulance with George for a little while. Then I got out again. You're walking around; you're aimless. Absolutely aimless. You go over and have a talk to Tommy, then talk to Harry; it's almost as though... you're isolated, in a sense.

"I phoned Jimmy's godparents, George and Krystyna. I thought, 'They're his godparents, they need to be here.' I phoned my brother – he's an undertaker up in Suffolk – and he was there before we went home, so we must have been outside the shop for a couple of hours.

"I was sitting on the kerb, and a stranger came up to me and said, 'I know who's done this. It's Jake Fahri.' Bear in mind Jake was known locally as a thug.

"Then the police tell you, 'Well, There's nothing more you can do, you might as well go home,' and you think, 'No, I mustn't. I've got to stay here.' They assured us they would let us know when they were going to bring Jimmy out."

. . . . . . . . . . . .

*So we went home, and on the way I was held by a friend, Teresa, whose own son had died through Sudden Adult Death Syndrome. I remember having her arms around me, leading me home, and sobbing, all the way home, trying to make sense of what had happened, and thinking, 'They're telling me my beautiful Jimmy's dead; he can't be dead.' Our house was full of people: Barry's mum had turned up, and his sister Dawn, and all our children and their friends – within a short time there were hundreds of people in our house and garden.*

"We'd gone home," Barry recalls, "and it's just awash with people coming and going, and at one stage I'm standing outside and the press were there. A *News of the World* reporter said, 'Have you got a picture of Jimmy?' so I went inside and grabbed the school photograph, taken just a few weeks before. They said, 'Tell us about Jimmy,' and I thought, 'Jimmy's a good boy, he must be portrayed properly.' Speaking to two reporters there, there's something strange: you're coping, working through this, there's a strength – something comes along to support you.

"One friend turned up, John, who's a great fellow; we've known him for many years and he loved Jimmy. I can see John now, coming along the road, and he could barely walk, he was sobbing so hard. He just fell into my arms, and I stood outside and we cried together. I'm telling him, 'All right, John, it's all right.' There's this strength that comes from somewhere.

"Then the police turned up, the Family Liaison Officer, a policewoman, and Detective Chief Inspector Cliff Lyons, who became a sort of leader to us, a colossus in our life. I remember saying to him, 'Do your best.' What a really stupid thing to say."

. . . . . . . . . . . .

The early evening is turning chilly on Burnt Ash Hill, still deserted, cordoned off at either end. A black private ambulance is parked outside the Three Cooks Bakery. On the opposite side of the road, watching, the father and mother stand, holding on to each other as the undertakers emerge from the bakery, carrying the long black body bag between them. On the other side of the ambulance doors stands a priest, his face pained with compassion for this family. Behind the parents, perhaps three dozen family members look on, scarcely able to believe that they are living this moment, inhabiting this drama. It all seems utterly surreal, and yet immediate – the undertakers have paused by the ambulance doors, the priest is praying now for Jimmy, for the repose of his soul. *How can he be praying for Jim,* thinks Tommy, *when he was alive and well only six hours ago? Tall, smiling, cheeky, loveable Jimmy, our little brother Jimbo – dead? There's Dad, leaning against the back of the ambulance, tears rolling down his face. There's Mum, leaning forward as if she wants to touch Jimmy. There's Tim, the head undertaker, who works with Dad's brother Uncle Terry. He's a seasoned pro, but he's in pieces.*

Passing his right hand in mid-air above Jimmy, making the sign of the cross, the priest prays, "Eternal rest grant unto him, O Lord, and may perpetual light shine upon him, and may he rest in peace."

As the doors are closed and the ambulance drives slowly away, a new wave of anguish surges over the father and mother, wrenched with yearning to see their son's face, touch his body, cradle him in their arms, to say goodbye… New pain… everything is new, strange now… new tears spring from their eyes, sobs choking, heaving from aching throats. The ambulance has almost disappeared at the bottom of the hill. Their son is gone. The father spreads his hands helplessly, winded by the shock, the wrongness of what is happening, breathless from the spasms of pain shuddering through his body.

Slowly, clinging to each other, sniffing, gasping, sobbing, or silent, the small crowd turns across the empty road and follows the parents at a respectful distance back to the house.

. . . . . . . . . . . . .

Further up Burnt Ash Hill, television cameras have been filming the ambulance as it pulled away. Barnie Choudhury is one of the first reporters on the scene. Against the backdrop of the empty street, with police officers standing vigil at the crime scene cordon, he gave the first account for BBC News: "It's not clear why Jimmy Mizen was inside this bakery store, but at 11.50 this morning there was a disturbance." A still shot of Jimmy, grinning cheerfully between two tailor's dummies, fills the screen. "It's thought he knew his attacker." Then there is a shot of a young couple crossing the road to place flowers by the bakery, negotiating with a policewoman at the cordon. "And during his short life, Jimmy made many friends who wanted to pay tribute to him."

One of his school friends, Conor, looking older than his sixteen years in suit and tie, says, "He was just such a lovely person. You know, walking to school, seeing him at school, playing games with him, all those… you know, primary school games, childhood memories that I'll never forget." He shakes his head, looks away. "All I can say is, I hope his family – I know his family well, Margaret and Barry, I just really hope that, you know, they stay strong and… all my prayers and thoughts are with them." He's unusually mature and articulate for his age.

The black private ambulance pulls away in the background. "A post-mortem examination will now be carried out on the dead teenager." Further up the hill, Barnie Choudhury speaks direct to camera: "The police don't believe that Jimmy Mizen's death was gang-related. Detectives are now speaking to local people, trying to piece together exactly what happened, and the motive behind this death."

Last, an interior shot of Our Lady of Lourdes church, where the parish priest, Father Edward Perera, leads a small congregation of local residents in prayer. "Tonight prayers were said for Jimmy and his family, who've been described as devout Catholics living in a close-knit community. Barnie Choudhury, BBC News, south-east London."

. . . . . . . . . . . .

*Harry was the main witness – this poor boy who was eighteen; he was traumatized. He had to be taken to the police station and had to take his clothes off to preserve any evidence. Not because they thought he was implicated, but they had to get the full picture quickly of what had gone on. We were all concerned, so a friend went down to pick him up for us. That evening, Harry started to go into shock. He was shaking, and we phoned a friend of ours who used to be our GP, Patrick Bentham, who came and spoke with Harry. I really wasn't sure what he could do, but I wanted Harry to get all the help he needed. I think I was expecting the GP to work miracles, but of course nothing could bring Jimmy back. All the medication in the world wasn't going to make things better.*

. . . . . . . . . . . . .

It's 3 a.m. The Mizen household is silent. The friends and neighbours have all gone home and the house is quiet. The sons and daughters have returned to their own rooms to sleep or try to sleep. Only the parents are still up. George is asleep in a makeshift bed on their bedroom floor. They are both exhausted but cannot think of sleep, cannot face retiring to their own bed, where they slept the night before, the last night when everything was normal. To go to bed now would seem somehow to be accepting what has happened. It's too soon to move to a new normal. *Our son died today, and now it's bedtime.*

Instead they have crept into Jimmy's room, to shelter in its dishevelled cosiness – his clothes on the floor, a guitar, CDs and magazines strewn here and there. To be in Jimmy's room, surrounded by Jimmy's things, is comforting. If only they could stay here, cocooned, not have to face the morning light, the neighbours and friends, the press, the noise of another day.

Standing at the window, Margaret looks out across the dark streets. The helicopter is approaching again, blades chugging louder and louder, glaring white search-beam raking the rooftops. It passes overhead, making the whole house shake. The overwhelming noise hammers through the silent house like a dentist's drill. The harsh light of the search beam pushes aside the dark, tearing huge holes in the night. *Maybe they've found him,* she thinks, *the boy who did this to my boy.* She feels almost nothing towards him. She probes her own feelings, puzzled. What does she feel? Weariness... a dread of noise and confrontation... *I suppose he'll have to be caught and locked away somewhere. That's what happens now, isn't it? More waste?* She would rather not have to think about him.

Barry sits on Jimmy's bed. His fingers stretch across the rumpled duvet. He imagines the recent touch of his son's hands, his son's feet, on these bedclothes. Just last night he was here. His face twitches, his eyes start with tears. *Where is Jimmy now? He should be here, warm in these sheets, safe, right here, as he was this time last night. Now he's lying in a cold morgue somewhere, zipped up in a bag, in a metal drawer? It can't be true. We were cuddling each other, me, Jimmy, and Margaret, just downstairs, just last night. Now he's gone, and we're left?*

He kicks off his shoes and stretches out, wrapping himself in Jimmy's duvet. Relief and release shake through him, welling from his eyes, a river bursting its banks, tears soaking into Jimmy's pillow, Jimmy's duvet, Jimmy's sheets. Jimmy's smell is all around him; his smiling face fills his mind. He feels safe and free, the father cradled in his son's embrace, and at last he sleeps.

. . . . . . . . . . . . .

The following morning, the Church of Our Lady of Lourdes is packed. Barry and Margaret have led their family to morning Mass, walking together past the place of Jimmy's death to the church where he was baptized. The journey is a kind of Via Dolorosa, and each step is anguish, with the eyes of their community and the press on them, making their private grief public. As they step outside, the front garden is awash with flowers. The compassion of friends and neighbours is overwhelming, wringing the heart. Fifty slow yards from Dallinger Road to Burnt Ash Hill, gathering breath, holding on to each other, then around the corner the bakery comes into view. Smashed windows, police tape cordon, and more flowers, bright flowers of early summer. The colours shout artlessly of life, youth, and vigour, like a slam in the guts. *Will we ever walk this way again and not think of Jimmy? Will it always feel this bad? Will it just become routine – that's the shop where Jimmy was killed?*

*Keep walking, hold my hand. Up the hill to church. I don't know if I can face it.*

They cross the road together and approach the church where Jimmy served as an altar boy and where – it strikes them suddenly

– his funeral will take place. It's like being in a play. We haven't read the script or learned our lines; we never knew we were on stage till it happened. What happens next?

Barry is due to serve that morning as a Eucharistic minister, one of four laypersons commissioned to serve the chalice during communion. The Eucharistic ministers stand at the front of the church, proffering the cup of consecrated wine to the worshippers as they process forward, and to each communicant they must pronounce the words, "the Blood of Christ". No one would have been surprised if Barry had chosen to step back from this role today, but by the time they arrive at church he has decided to go through with it. It feels like the right thing to do.

The impact is profound. Almost everyone in church is weeping, as they queue up to receive communion, as they cluster around Margaret and her children to hold their hands, hug them, kiss them, touch them. Afterwards, the Mizens move amongst the congregation, thanking them, reassuring them, comforting the grieving, shocked community – We're here, we're all right, it will be all right.

"You've got this strength," says Barry. "For some reason, part of you is trying to help other people through this. You're very concerned with how other people are dealing with this. People are crying, I'm cuddling them – my shirt was wet afterwards – and I thought, 'This is ridiculous. You're supposed to be cuddling me!' We're actually being, if you like, the strong people there."

As they come out of the church after Mass, the press are gathering, waiting for them.

"I didn't expect the press to be there," Margaret recalls. "We didn't plan it. Why would they be there? Why would they know where we went to church, and indeed what time Mass we went to? We just had no idea. They started asking us questions, and to this day, I believe the words that came out of our mouths were God's words. I spoke about the parents of the boy that had killed Jimmy. It made headlines about forgiveness."

"We have such happy memories of Jimmy," she said to the crowd of reporters. "I remember holding him in my arms when he was born, but you know, the parents of the boy who killed our son, they also held him as a baby when he was born. They must also have been so happy when their son was born. We have such happy memories of Jimmy, but what do they have? Only the memory of this terrible thing their son has done. All I can say is, my prayers are with them. Anger breeds anger and bitterness, and that's what killed our son. I will not go down that road, of being angry."

"What we felt," says Barry, "is – what if the police turned up and said, 'One of your sons has just murdered somebody,' how would we feel? We'd feel absolutely devastated."

"We came out of church, and the words came out – I hadn't prepared anything to say because I didn't know I had to," says Margaret. "God moves us in mysterious ways."

. . . . . . . . . . . . .

Back in Dallinger Road, the BBC reporter Barnie Choudhury was waiting at Rob Clifford's house, next-door to the Mizens', in the hope of an interview. Writing for the BBC's in-house magazine a week later, he describes the encounter:

I have done hundreds of "death-knocks" in my 27 years. Barry and Margaret Mizen were at morning mass at their local Catholic church. So Chris Parkinson, my camera crew, and I were seated drinking coffee with their next-door neighbour, Rob Clifford. I asked him to speak to the Mizens on my behalf.

Five minutes later they walked through his door. They looked frail, vulnerable, and you sensed that the shock had not yet hit them. So when Margaret Mizen said: "You did the report last night, thank you," I choked a bit. I wanted to walk away. It did not feel right. I felt like a used car salesman about to cheat a decent couple by pretending to be their friend and giving them the deal of their lives. But she continued: "You really brought Jimmy's character across well. It was our Jimmy you described. How can we help you?"

In the interview, Margaret and Barry take turns to speak, passing the baton instinctively as the other is lost for words or unable to speak. Eyes downcast, weeping, Margaret says, "Jimmy was just the sweetest boy you could ever meet. Happy all the time, whistled as he walked down the road." She pauses, searching her memories. "You know, as a baby, he had meningitis, and he managed to get through that without any…" She smiles, almost laughing, and turns to Barry. "He managed to get through it, and he sailed through life, happy…" She sighs. "I don't know what to say… such a wonderful boy…"

"Jimmy was very content with his life," says Barry, taking over. "He was very content with his family. He loved his family. His family loved him. Jimmy was able to express that love as well: he'd give me a kiss when I dropped him off at school. You don't see too many teenagers do that. Jimmy was full of confidence. An innate decency ran through Jimmy's body. A decent, fine young feller…" His voice cracks slightly. "Protective of other people… protective of, maybe, the weak, if that's not a silly thing to say." Tears spring in his eyes. He shakes his head, blinks, searches for words: "He loved, erm… he loved…"

"Protective of his family," says Margaret.

"Friends have described him as a 'gentle giant'," says Barnie Choudhury. "Is that how you'd describe him?"

They both smile. "He's certainly sprung up recently, hasn't he?" says Barry, grinning to Margaret. "Gentle always. Giant recently."

"He's just grown and grown and grown," says Margaret. "And our boys are all different sizes, and there'd be such a lot of joshing between them – 'Oh, you're a midget', 'Oh, you're too big, look at you!' And they used to play games on the Wii, in our garage, and whoever lost would have to make the tea, and it was usually Jimmy. And I can hear 'em now – 'Go on, Jim, make the tea!' The camaraderie between them was amazing. Oh gosh!" She shakes her head. "What a loss! What a loss to this world!"

At another point in the interview, asked about Jake Fahri, she says, "I feel for the parents of this boy. I don't know why, I can't get them out of my mind, because what's happened to Jimmy is the worst thing possible, but we've got such wonderful memories. They haven't got wonderful memories for their son. All they can think about is the evil he's done. My prayers are with the family, that's all I can say. I can't, I don't, feel anger."

Barnie Choudhury's article continues:

> You know instinctively when you have a good interview. This one, for me, ranked as exceptional. We even managed to persuade one of their sons to download private, moving pictures of Jimmy onto a DVD. No other media outlet had those party pictures for twenty-four hours. I left thinking: this is the definitive interview. It is fifteen minutes long and because we are "one BBC", everyone has access to it. On the Monday, one producer who works on the Ten described it as "one of the seminal interviews of the year, like Stephen Lawrence's parents". A senior manager kindly sent a touching email.

In gauging the likely impact Margaret and Barry would have on viewers, Barnie Choudhury was absolutely right. This interview would ignite a storm of media interest and inspire an extraordinary reaction of admiration and solidarity across the country and beyond.

Speaking that same day at the Global Day of Prayer held at Millwall Football Club, the Mizen family club, the newly elected Mayor of London, Boris Johnson, said, "In the last few days we have seen the deaths of Lyle Tulloch and Jimmy Mizen, and I'm sure their parents will be in our prayers. There are too many parents across London today who have lost their young children or young teenagers in the last year to gun crime and knife crime... together we can do something and together we must do something and together we will do something."

Within days, letters, tributes, and gifts were arriving from every part of the UK, including one from 10 Downing Street. In his letter of 13 May, Prime Minister Gordon Brown wrote:

I also wanted to say how struck I was by your profound comments about your happy memories of your son, which you contrasted with the feelings of the parents of his murderer. Jimmy's killing is a shocking event and it should make us all pause; but Jimmy's life is also a testament to goodness and decency – he helps us remember that most young people are honest and law-abiding and gives a pattern for others to follow.

My thoughts are with you,

Yours sincerely
Gordon Brown

And, the following day, to match the Prime Minister's letter, the Conservative leader David Cameron wrote:

As a parent, I simply cannot imagine the sheer horror and heartache of losing a child, especially in such a brutal and meaningless way. This terrible crime will have shocked every parent in the country...

I was particularly moved by the way you have handled this appalling tragedy – especially your refusal to give in to what would be entirely understandable anger...

That you were so quick to sympathize with the family of Jimmy's killer – describing how, unlike them, your family will have only happy memories of your son – was heartbreaking in its generosity...

Yours sincerely
David Cameron

Handwritten letters arrived from Boris Johnson, from the Mayor of Lewisham Steve Bullock, from the Leader of Greenwich Council Chris Roberts, and from the local MP Bridget Prentice all testify to a similar depth of feeling and concern, and admiration for the Mizens' public witness of courage and faith.

A passage from Bridget Prentice's letter is worthy of note:

> I also want to pass on the sympathy and condolence of many of my colleagues who, in the last few days, have sought me out to express their sadness for you at losing Jimmy and also their admiration for you all as a family. Your example is one they wish to emulate. I have also had emails from around the country from people just wishing you peace and I thought it important I passed this on to you.

Later in the letter she gives her home telephone number with an open invitation to contact her at any point for help.

Some of the most striking letters are from members of the public unknown to the family:

> A message to the Mizen Family
>
> … you are to me an amazing family and a shining example, not only to Lee, but to the world at large… Each member of your family would have been excused being, at the very least, angry towards the person who robbed you… of your son but you chose to be bigger than that…
>
> … you hold the brightest light in the world at the moment…
>
> As a father of a five-year-old, I only pray that my reaction would be similar to yours… you are right; anger does not solve anything. I do want to say, though, that I feel much safer with people in the world like you and your remarkably humane family.
>
> From a local resident

Dear Margaret & Barry Mizen,

You will have to forgive me as I am not accustomed to writing
letters to people I do not know… From first seeing Margaret
on the news talking about Jimmy and your feelings towards
the boy who took him away from you, I have the greatest
respect for you and your views.

I could not quite believe that you can genuinely feel no
anger or bitterness towards someone that had torn your
family apart in that way… He has not torn your family apart,
because you won't let him do that; you and your family are
stronger than his attempt to do that…

… I just wanted you to know you have also given strength
and belief to ordinary people too.

Many people see forgiveness as a sign of weakness;
you prove that this is not the case. You are truly one of the
strongest, most courageous families I have witnessed in my life.

Thank you and God bless you.
Victoria x
Leicestershire

Dear Jimmy's mum & dad,

I want to tell you that your lovely son's personality shone
through his lovely face. I heard your son, Danny, speaking
on the Jeremy Vine show the other day, and listening to him
speaking so bravely, brought me to tears. Your dignity, and
Danny's ability to speak on the radio, given his heartache, are
a credit to you and your family…

… we, as mothers and fathers, all across our country, are
thinking of you with love, with concern…

My love to you,
Sue Standley

. . . . . . . . . . . .

The same spirit of sympathy was embodied movingly by the visit of their former parish priest, Father Barry, the day after Jimmy's death. "He stood there, crying," says Barry. "And that was so lovely. No pious words. He's crying with us. That's what we needed."

"Sister Rita arrived, who had been the head teacher for my older children at primary school," Margaret recalls. "It was wonderful to see her – I felt comforted by that! She knew us so well from all those years ago, but she said the right things. She asked us, 'Do you feel a little bit of joy?'"

"You know, it was strange," says Barry, "in amongst it all, there was a tiny bit of joy. Where does that come from? What sense does that make? She said, 'That's Jimmy from heaven. That's God letting you know that Jimmy's in heaven.'"

A letter from another nun, Sister Kathleen, writing a week later from Massachusetts, USA, ended with these words:

> Jimmy is praying for you now, for your family – and will be a friend from heaven to all of us.

. . . . . . . . . . . .

Margaret began the next day, Monday 12 May, with an early morning telephone interview for the Victoria Derbyshire show on BBC Radio 5 Live. "It was a very difficult interview," Margaret recalls. "I felt I was being judged on my faith. I felt it was the wrong context to be questioned in that way. I said, 'We choose to believe in a good God.' It felt wrong to be put on the spot in that way, as a newly bereaved mother."

After this, the family attended the farewell Mass for Year Eleven students at Jimmy's school, St Thomas More. This had been a difficult year for staff and students; two children had been killed in a car accident on New Year's Day and, following this weekend's news, the mood was one of shocked disbelief. Margaret and Barry were asked to speak by the head teacher and, as they had the day before at church, they stepped forward instinctively to comfort and encourage the distressed teenagers.

Many notes and letters arrived from Jimmy's school friends over the following days, referring specifically to this moment:

To Mizen family

Jimmy was a great person. He's with God now and is still always going to be happy. Thank you for making this easier for us. We all loved Jim. He was our Big Friendly Giant.

xxx Rick

To Barry & Margaret

I am writing to thank you. Thank you for Jimmy. Nothing's the same without Jimbo. He did so many things that made my day. Either him cracking a joke, hurting himself or even locking himself on the train. There will only ever be one Jimbo Mizen. No one compares to him and the great person he was and always will be. He called me the Joker but he was the true clown. I respect you so much as a family. I even used your words in my exam. I had to write about "Jesus' teaching on forgiveness" and I quoted "Anger breeds anger". Hopefully you'll get me an A!

I got this plant for you called "Happy Times" as I will always remember the good times with Jim and I know you will too.

Thanks again,
Sean Gibbs x

Hi, Jimmy's family

I would just like to share with you the biggest memory
of Jimmy I had, and that was he was always smiling. He
will be missed for ever but I know that wherever he is he
will still be smiling.

Love Amy

Beneath this she has drawn a little cartoon figure of Jimmy, with a
big smile on his face and a floating heart, with an arrow pointing to
him, saying "Jim xxx".

Jimmy

If you were to sit in the shadow of a tree
Would you know the shadow to be Jimmy?
Sheltering you from the sun's cruel rays,
And wanting you to know he's never far away.
If you were to stare at the clouds in the sky
Would you not see Jimmy in each that passed by?
Watching your tears fall to the ground,
And hoping you know he'll always be around.

Next time you look at any innate thing
Look closer and you'll see
Jimmy's heart is within.

Love Sorrelle
Xxx

Hundreds of Jimmy's schoolmates signed one of his shirts with
messages and prayers of love, sorrow, and support. Again, as
Margaret and Barry emerged from the school, they were asked to
speak to the press, who were there in force. "How are you coping?"

asked one of the reporters. "How do you think I cope?" Margaret replied. "Because I have a faith, and I believe that my son is safe."

"I think I got a bit cocky, a little bit clever there," Margaret recalls, with some embarrassment, "but they never ridiculed us for that, thank God. I think there was just a sense of hope for everyone."

. . . . . . . . . . . . .

*We went later that day to identify Jimmy's body formally at the public mortuary. We were absolutely desperate to see him. The Coroner's Office would only allow immediate family to view the body, which meant me and Barry, our children, and our grandson James. So long-term partners of his siblings, who all knew Jimmy, weren't allowed in. It was really sad. But at the back of our minds, we had our plan to have Jimmy's body home before the funeral, to have an open coffin in the front room. In retrospect, if we'd known what was going to happen, we would have insisted on a lot more viewings of Jimmy's body.*

*We went to the public mortuary with our Family Liaison Officer, Kerry. We were shown into a large room, and at one end was a large glass screen, and on the other side was Jimmy's body on a table. I honestly don't know what I was expecting, but my first reaction was, he's so long. He looked so long. But he looked scared. There was definitely a look on his face of fear. I think because of the speed of his death, the fact that the blood left his body so quickly, there were no bruises or marks of any kind. Our family email address is barrymiz12 – that's the nine children, our grandson James, plus me and Barry. So we were the barrymiz eleven, and the twelfth was behind the glass screen. We couldn't touch him. We weren't allowed a great deal of time. I don't know how long we stayed with him. It didn't seem that long.*

*After I'd gone out with all the children, Barry was left there, still sitting there with James. He was just leaning there, looking. He said, "Grandad, I can't go. I can't leave him, Grandad."*

*We weren't worried about having to leave, because we thought we'd be allowed to come back again and see him. They promised us – they absolutely promised us – they would look after him and that we would be able to see him again, and they let us down. I've read about other families, who were allowed to go back and see their loved ones every day. Why weren't we? Because we*

*didn't push for it; we did as we were told. I always tend to do what I'm told—*
*"the right thing", but in hindsight, I have many, many regrets about that.*

*I longed to hold him. I suppose I felt despair. Most of the time, I don't
think I slept in that week. I'd be sitting up in our front room, at two, three,
four in the morning sometimes. Trying to make sense of it. The only sense that
came to me at that time was that God was ready for my son – and that gave
me comfort. I was determined we would not let it destroy our family, because
enough damage was done. I longed to hold him, and I couldn't. But having
George and Samantha and the others was our strength. We would sit around
our kitchen table, and talk and laugh about Jimmy, so it wasn't all tears.
(There were lots of tears.) Sometimes, I'd be upstairs in the bedroom, and the
tears would come, but it wasn't a case of wanting to die.*

*We'd be lying in bed, stupid hours, in the middle of the night, and Barry
would ask me, "Are you awake yet?" and I'd say, "Yes, I can't sleep either."
We'd pray, and cry, and hold each other, in those dark times, and tell each
other we knew he was safe. But I never felt the anger that everyone expected
me to feel. People couldn't really understand my reaction. I was never ridiculed
for it, but most people said, "I wouldn't be like that, if it was my son." But
you want to say to people, "You don't know how you're going to behave! No
one knows!" I didn't know, but I do think in a way it was part of the grace
that God had given me, and I think perhaps it was a miracle. I felt absolute
sadness, beyond belief, and the pain of thinking of Jimmy and the fear that
he went through – because from the time that piece of glass severed his artery,
he must have been so fearful, and it showed on his face. But I couldn't work
up the anger.*

*I was with Joanne one day, and I said, "I feel a bit angry today; do you?"
She said yes, so we went in the garden and said, "What shall we do?" We
had some drinks in our hands, so we threw the mugs, but they bounced off the
grass, and we ended up rolling around laughing.*

*People would say, "You don't feel angry now, but you will." But I don't.
If I think about Jake Fahri, I don't feel anger. I just feel sadness. I was
always determined that I would not sink. I will always cope, and I have
coped. I have days when I feel miserable and think, "I've got to pick myself
up again and do my housework and make dinner," and I don't always want
to. But back then, my brother was around our house a lot, and he took control*

*of things like the telephone, and I was so grateful for that. Danny's girlfriend Fay would always make sure I had something to eat, and Barry's sister Dawn came and made endless cups of tea.*

*In the times when I'd be crying, and felt despair, the moment I started praying, it was as if my body went into something else, almost. Something was there, and I felt something around me, God's loving arms, I don't know. But I definitely felt a strength that lifted me up, on the days when I didn't want to get out of bed – I felt I was almost being lifted out of bed. You can say these things but not believe it, but I really, really felt God's presence there, all the way through, and I still do. I can't honestly say that life's always easy. It isn't. But when I feel the deepest, darkest moments, I feel again almost like arms on me, lifting me, guiding me. I don't know. Well I do know.*

*Barry says he would "cry his heart out" and say, "Lord, no more. You've taken one. Please don't take another. What's happening to this family? We've done nothing wrong in life, we've done the right thing…" But each time he felt overwhelmed by what happened to Jimmy, he would pray the Hail Mary, and straight away, he said, a relief would run through his body, every time, this instant physical relief from the physical pain of grief. He said the pain would well up on the inside of his stomach, a pain that gripped him, like being folded in half and wound up in a vice. That's how he describes it. He'd think, "I want to cry," and he'd pray the Hail Mary, and he'd be clear. But every so often he says he feels overwhelmed by pity. He feels incredibly sorry for Jimmy. "Poor little fella," he says. "Sixteen years of age… and that awful fear. Hiding in a cupboard because you're so scared."*

*Before Barry and I did anything, at that time – and we still do this – we prayed together. We'd pray together and say, "Lord, let it be Your words that we speak." I believe they were. I'm not academic or particularly articulate, but undoubtedly the words we were saying were the right words, because things were being picked up.*

. . . . . . . . . . . . .

*Things were being picked up.* Any murder involves the victim's family in the drama of public investigations, inquests, and court proceedings, but now the brutal death of a blameless teenager, and his parents' response, was becoming a story that seemed to be touching the heart of the nation. For weeks on end, the family was sustained by the gifts of food and drink brought round by friends and neighbours. The local council sent daily waste collections to their home to take away the rubbish generated by all the visitors and gifts. Dozens of bouquets of flowers continued to arrive every day, along with other gifts and donations. For the memorial service the following weekend, the local Scouts group erected a marquee in Barry and Margaret's garden, while Marks & Spencer and Sainsbury's provided free food and drink.

Church leaders started speaking of them as "ambassadors of faith", politicians cited their inspiring example of citizenship and community spirit, individuals from all over the country and across the world were writing to thank Margaret and Barry for touching their lives at a deep level. Hundreds of commemorative Masses were said for Jimmy. A handmade shawl was sent from a group called Knitting People Together based in Liverpool, in which each stitch represented a prayer for Jimmy and his family, and for peace. The Govan Chairman sent a beautiful miniature chair made from olive wood from the Holy Land, interwoven with wood reclaimed from antique church pews, with Jimmy's name carved into the back with exquisite workmanship. A new bright yellow rose was cultivated in Jimmy's memory, the Jimmy Mizen Rose. The Vrede Olive Tree Plantation in South Africa dedicated an olive tree to Jimmy. Leathermarket JMB launched the Jimmy Mizen Apprenticeship Scheme later that summer.

The memorial service the following weekend was attended by more than 500 people, many of whom had to stand outside in the rain; extra speakers were set up to relay the service to those outside. Speaking to the press afterwards, Barry said, "I don't want some politician saying, 'That was a terrible crime; we need to change the law. We'll solve this problem overnight. Job done.' I don't want my son forgotten about. We need to ask ourselves, do we need more laws? Or do we need to ask ourselves what values we want to live by?" Already, just one week after Jimmy's death, Barry and Margaret were finding that simply by answering truthfully the barrage of media questions

*Above*: Jimmy aged 3 months on a family picnic in Hastings, August 1992.

*Above, from left to right*: Harry (3), Jimmy (3 months), and Tommy (10).

*Left*: Jimmy aged 3 and Harry aged 6. Jimmy hadn't started school, but he wanted to dress like Harry.

*Top*: Margaret's niece's wedding 2002. Back row – Joanne, Tommy, Barry, Margaret, George, James, Bobby, Billy. Front row – Harry, Samantha, Jimmy.

*Above*: Jimmy (6) and Harry (9) in their Millwall shirts.

*Above*: Jimmy's first day at St Winifred's School, April 1997.

*Above*: Danny aged 25 and Jimmy aged 12 at Jimmy's confirmation.

*Left*: Jimmy and Barry at Jimmy's confirmation.

*Below*: Jimmy (11), Danny (24), and Harry (13) at Sidcup Rugby club.

*Above*: Jimmy at 14 on a Rugby tour.

*Right*: Jimmy winning the street party fancy dress competition for the Queen's Golden Jubilee in 2002, aged 11.

*Below*: Jimmy (14) and Harry (16) at a family gathering.

*Left*: Jimmy (14), Billy (26), Samantha (20), Barry, Harry (16), and Danny (28) in the family garden.

*Right*: Jimmy aged 14 gardening at home.

*Left*: Barry, Jimmy (15), Margaret, and George (8) on holiday in France.

*Left*: Bobby aged 24 and Jimmy aged 15 at Samantha's 21st birthday.

*Below*: George and Jimmy on holiday in France in 2007.

*Bottom*: Jimmy aged 15 at New Dawn Conference in Walsingham.

*Left*: Jimmy with Margaret at Samantha's 21st birthday party.

*Below*: Jimmy aged 15 and George aged 8 outside Ciy Hall in London.

*Bottom*: Jimmy and Samantha at her birthday party.

*Top*: Jimmy, Margaret, George, and Barry on holiday in France in 2007.

*Above*: Barry, Danny (29), Margaret, Jimmy (15), and Samantha (21) at Sidcup Rugby Club.

*Left*: Margaret aged 6 winning Miss Junior Lovely in 1958.

thrown at them, they in turn were provoking searching questions about the vision and values of British society.

Perhaps the most telling testimony to their remarkable impact is Barnie Choudhury's letter to their next-door neighbour Rob Clifford:

21 May 2008

Dear Rob,

I wanted to thank you for your kindness and help a week ago last Sunday. Sometimes our job can be deeply unpleasant. We come across as vultures without soul.

But the interview with Barry and Margaret has haunted me ever since.

When I am asked the question: what is your most memorable interview – then I will say, the Mizens.

I hoped I had sensitivity before – but I know this has irrevocably changed my outlook.

I found myself not getting angry with a motorist who cut me up; I am finding that I can be and should be more tolerant of my neighbours' kids knocking their ball incessantly into our garden.

Quite a change. Quite an influence.

The Mizens are remarkable people – and since meeting them there hasn't been a day that I have not thought about them, wishing I could throw a protective shield around them...

Once the trial starts, then I know it'll begin all over again. But for the moment I hope the press will allow the family to grieve in peace.

All the best,
Barnie

This, from a seasoned career journalist, a "veteran hack" of twenty-seven years' experience, winner of the Media Personality of the Year Award, is astonishing. Because of meeting Margaret and Barry, he wants to be a better, more generous person. Writing to grant permission for the use of this material, he said, "Every year on May 10th, I say a prayer for the Mizens and hold my daughter a little bit closer." Barnie now says that he traces his eventual decision to leave the BBC to this life-shaping encounter with the shoe-mender from Lewisham and his wife.

# 6

# The Funeral

Jimmy's funeral took place on Friday 20 June 2008.

*We'd planned to hold a traditional pre-funeral wake in the family home. We wanted to do what we did with my mum: to have an open coffin in the house, all gathered round, say prayers in the room, do what we needed to do. That's what we had in our heads for Jimmy.*

*But on 10 June we received a telephone call from the embalmers advising us against an open coffin, as the condition of Jimmy's body had deteriorated significantly. Some mistake had been made, apparently, with the care of Jimmy's body at the public mortuary between the first police post-mortem and the second, independent post-mortem conducted for the benefit of the counsel for the defence. Later on, in our letter to the Coroner's Office, we wrote:*

> This felt like a second bereavement. We were very much looking forward to seeing Jimmy and paying respects and saying goodbye to our darling son. It is very important to our family to have an open coffin in order to say our prayers and goodbyes. We had planned to have Jimmy at home Thursday night before the funeral but now we can't. This is normal practice in our family and we have done so with other family members that have passed away. We believe that not being able to see Jimmy is due to unnecessary and careless delays. Because of this we as a whole family suffered what seemed to us to be a second bereavement. It was a very difficult day and caused the family much grief and pain, which we are still suffering with.

*The undertaker said they couldn't really do anything, even though they'd been working on him all day. He said in his opinion the body had been left out overnight in the mortuary. Apparently, when the second post-mortem was due to take place, on 28 May, the defence pathologist had failed to turn up. The following day he suddenly turned up and they did the second post-mortem. Anyway, in the end, my brother, our son Billy, Joanne, and grandson James went to view the body. James said afterwards he wished he hadn't.*

*It was the most painful day, worse than the day Jimmy was killed. Everyone was coming to us, crying and crying. It was an awful day. My brother and the others will have to live with those mental images. We felt he had not been looked after. The pain that he'd been neglected, and seeing the pain in the children's eyes – we were all crying. I wanted to touch him again. I regret not touching him in the baker's. We needed the chance to pay our last respects with dignity. It was important for us to pray with Jimmy, and it hurt so much that we were denied that opportunity. I remember our last words to the lady at the mortuary, after what transpired to be our only viewing: "Please, please look after him."*

*Recently, a friend's daughter has offered to do a painting of Jimmy – and there is so much expectation that we are going to see him. We are so looking forward to seeing a new image of Jimmy. I think it's the same thing with an open coffin. Yes, the person is dead, but you are looking forward to seeing him again, one more time. In the end we had a closed wicker coffin surrounded with beautiful yellow and white flowers, to represent this vibrant young man, and we then had the prayers the morning of the funeral, and that was so important. The wicker coffin was brought into the front room with yellow and white roses – the papal colours! – but it looked right. The funeral was planned meticulously, largely by Tommy. He had chosen songs, not hymns, and I was quite worried the priest wouldn't approve, but as it turned out it was absolutely right. The whole funeral was beautiful.*

. . . . . . . . . . . . .

In the television news coverage, the sun is shining on a large crowd walking slowly up Burnt Ash Hill, following a hearse decked in flowers. Flanked by his family, Jimmy's younger brother George leads the crowd, carrying a large black and white framed portrait of Jimmy. The grainy photograph pictures him sitting on a football in his Millwall shirt, aged seven, grinning all over his impish face.

On the pavement close to the Three Cooks Bakery stands the now-iconic school portrait shot of Jimmy in tie and blazer, surrounded by white and yellow chrysanthemums. At its foot, a beautiful hand-woven carpet is spread, covered with votive candles, lanterns and flowers, and a statue of the Virgin Mary. The railings behind are draped with the flag of St George, and the emblems of Millwall Football Club, Sidcup Rugby Club, and the local Scouts' group, of which Jimmy used to be a member. Next to this, framed by the school ties of dozens of Jimmy's friends, knotted around the railings, a large hand-painted poster is mounted:

> THERE ARE THREE THINGS
> THAT LAST FOR EVER:
> FAITH, HOPE,
> AND LOVE;
> THE GREATEST OF THESE IS LOVE

The Church of Our Lady of Lourdes is thronged with a huge congregation. Family, friends and neighbours, staff, pupils and governors from Jimmy's primary and secondary schools, representatives and officials of the nationwide Catholic community, and local dignitaries – hundreds have gathered to pay tribute to Jimmy and say farewell.

The Sri Lankan parish priest, Father Edward Pereira, welcomes the huge congregation. "We are here to celebrate the life and works of Jimmy," he says. The opening hymn, "I Watch the Sunrise", has a thoughtful, slightly melancholy quality, offset by the strength and energy with which it is sung. After a silence, Father Edward prays:

"Lord God, source and destiny of our lives, in Your loving Providence You gave us Jimmy, to grow in wisdom, age, and grace. Now You have called him to Yourself. As we grieve the loss of one so young, we seek to understand Your purpose."

Barry stands to deliver the first reading, from 2 Corinthians. He reads it slowly and calmly, containing not only his own emotion, but also the palpable intensity of feeling in the church:

"Brothers, we wish you happiness; try to grow perfect; help one another. Be united; live in peace, and the God of love and peace will be with you. Greet one another with the holy kiss. All the saints send you greetings. The grace of the Lord Jesus Christ, the love of God and the fellowship of the Holy Spirit be with you all."

The congregation sings a setting of Psalm 91, "You who dwell in the shelter of the Lord". In this ancient song of devotion, the psalmist praises the protective power of God, "my refuge, my rock, in whom I trust", shielding him from the many dangers that beset him: famine, the terror of the night, the arrow that flies by day – "though thousands fall about you, near you it shall not come, for to His angels He's given a command to guard you in all of your ways." In this setting, there is an inescapable poignancy to these words. The refrain has particular significance for Margaret:

And He will raise you up on eagle's wings,
Bear you on the breath of dawn,
Make you to shine like the sun
And hold you in the palm of His hand.

"I had a vision of Jimmy being lifted up to heaven on the palm of God's hand," she recalls, "and this refrain captured it beautifully."

The Bible reading that follows, the story of Lazarus from St John's Gospel, expresses the cry of the faithful believer to a seemingly absent God: where were You when I needed You?

Now Father Edward stands to preach; no easy task, with such a huge, diverse gathering – young, old, and in between, believers of all faiths and none – at an occasion of such intense grief. He paints the scene from the gospel story movingly: Jesus arriving in the village of Bethany, and Martha running to greet Him, full of hurt and confusion, full of sorrow for her brother Lazarus's untimely death, hurling the reproach, "If You had been here, my brother would not have died."

"We offer comfort to the Mizen family today," says Father Edward, "as Jesus offered it to Martha and Mary: 'Your brother will live,' He says. 'I am the Resurrection and the Life. If anyone believes in me, even though he dies he will live, and whoever lives and believes in me will never die.' Lovingly, with great compassion, He asks her, 'Do you believe this?' and she replies, 'Yes, Lord, I believe.' To the Mizens, in your pain and your loss, He says to you right now, 'Your son, your brother Jimmy – will live.'"

A little later in his address, Father Edward turns in the pulpit and speaks gently to the family: "Margaret and Barry, dear friends, just as you have lived your faith so wonderfully during these painful days, do continue to live that faith, and I promise you that God will give you deep and inner peace, and the comfort that you need. No one can give that."

He concludes by quoting from the celebrated Catholic writer Henri Nouwen's book *Life of the Beloved*: "The first response to brokenness is to face it squarely and befriend it. The second response is to put it under the blessing." Nouwen tries to explain what this might mean by describing a scene from Leonard Bernstein's opera *Mass*, in which a grief-stricken priest kneels amid a scene of devastation next to a broken communion chalice and says, "I never realized that broken glass could shine so brightly."

"I think these words capture the mystery of Jimmy's life," says Father Edward, "and the life of every Christian of faith. Margaret and Barry, you've said many a time that something good will come out of this sadness, and that will come true. May God bless you, Barry and Margaret, and Jimmy's brothers and sisters, may God be your strength and comfort."

"Father Edward really rose to the occasion," Margaret recalls. "He managed to embrace the spectrum of people there and the intensity of emotion. He did justice to the complexity of our faith. There are no easy answers."

"Eternal rest grant unto him, O Lord, and may perpetual light shine upon him, and may he rest in peace" – the words of the ancient prayer "Requiem Aeternam" end the sermon, and a group of friends and neighbours come forward to lead the prayers of intercession. The congregation stands to sing "I Will Raise You Up", a setting of the words of Jesus from the story of Lazarus.

And now Jimmy's favourite song is playing: Coldplay's tender, searing anthem "Fix You", which was the most played song on his laptop, as sixteen of his friends process forward carrying lit candles, one for each year of his life, and place them around his coffin.

> Tears stream down your face
> When you lose something you cannot replace…
>
> Lights will guide you home
> And ignite your bones
> And I will try
> To fix you.

The family's tributes to Jimmy are led bravely by George, who describes his brother as "a nice boy, the nicest you could ever meet". He introduces each of Jimmy's siblings and his nephew by name, and concludes with simple brevity: "He was a very special boy. He was sixteen."

In his own tribute, Barry quotes from the Holocaust survivor Victor Frankl's book *Man's Search for Meaning*:

> We cannot judge a biography by its length, by the number of pages in it. We must judge it by the richness of its contents. Sometimes the "unfinished" are among the most beautiful symphonies.

He speaks of Jimmy's baptism as a baby, how they gave thanks for him then, and how they give thanks again for him now, for everything that his life has brought to them and to the world. He speaks of his pleasure at seeing so many young people present, and how we should be proud of them and nurture them. He speaks fondly of Jimmy's smile – "People write to us and say what they remember of Jimmy is his smile," – and he shares some funny memories: whistling together on their way to work, Jimmy's love of food. "In the morning, he liked his sleep, and he tended to go to bed before me on a school day, and he'd put his head round the door and I knew what was coming: 'Lift in the morning, Dad?' I said, 'Sure.' 'Goodnight, Dad.' 'Goodnight, son. God bless you, son.' 'And you, Dad.' That's precious."

"I don't have any regrets about anything we spoke about. Everything we said was great. I don't wish I'd said any more – maybe for longer – and I don't wish I'd said any less. He was a lovely boy."

Because Jimmy loved ties as a little boy, Barry explains, each of his children will present their brother with ties that represent different parts of Jimmy's life. George takes out the tie of his primary school, St Winifred's, where Jimmy also went, and loops it around one of the handles of the wicker coffin.

Next, Samantha walks to the front with one of her teachers, who helps her to present a series of pictures she's made to express her tribute: photographs of Jimmy on holiday and Jimmy dancing at her twenty-first birthday party. Her teacher explains, "Sam said that he was a very good dancer. She's drawn a picture of Jimmy mowing the lawn, a picture of the two of them together, brother and sister, and finally of herself waving goodbye." Underneath this last picture she has designed a glittering star. To sustained applause, Samantha takes one of Barry's old ties, which Jimmy used to wear, and ties it to the coffin.

Billy and Harry step up next. "When you move away from home," says Billy, "one of the things that keep you going is when people ask you about your family. I always enjoy talking about them, and you often get asked how many brothers and sisters you have. I always used to love saying I have six brothers and two sisters and I also have a nephew. After Jimmy's death, I went back to work and a lady asked me how many brothers and sisters I have, and I had no idea how to answer it. So I just shied away from the question. Then, talking about it with my brother Danny a couple of weeks ago, we both agreed that whenever I'm asked that question again, I will always, always say that I have six brothers and two sisters and a nephew, and Jimmy will always, always come after Harry and before George, for ever."

Harry holds up the Millwall Football Club tie, explaining Jimmy's affection for their "family club", and ties it on the coffin as applause breaks out again.

Next up is Danny, showing his Sidcup Rugby Club "Hundred" tie. "When you've played a hundred games for the First team, you get presented with this tie; it's quite a big deal. It means a lot to me, it's really precious, but not as precious as Jimmy. What has amazed me about Jimmy is the stories that have come out in the last six weeks, stories that I never even knew about, helping the lady round the corner with her shopping, feeding the homeless guy, just because he wanted to, helping others, respecting others, being there for his friends. For a boy so young, a young man, it's truly amazing. I say to Jimmy: 'Jim, I'm always gonna miss you, always love you, never forget you. Most of all, I'm always gonna be proud to be your brother. Love you, mate.'" Another burst of applause.

"Since Jimmy died," says Bobby, "people have asked me, 'How do you do it? How do you get through it? How are you so strong?' I don't think I am, but with Jimmy's memory, and the love we have for Jimmy, he's really got us through it. Not a day goes by that I don't think of him, and I know for evermore that I will do, every day. Losing a brother so young is a thing I never thought would happen, it's the hardest thing I've ever had to do, but the memories we have of Jimmy are just amazing: his caring, giving spirit. He was a beautiful person, and we will always love him for ever. The tie I have is from St Thomas More. My parents have been involved in this school for nineteen years. It's a big part of our life, and although Jimmy wasn't particularly academic, he loved the school. He had some great friends there, and it means a lot to us all."

James begins his tribute in a jaunty tone: "I want to start off and tell you about the tie. This is the Scouts' tie. We all once went to Scouts, which Jimmy liked. I think he went. Did he go? I'm sure he did go." Laughter ripples across the congregation. "We all went. I'm not going to come up here and talk to you about Jimmy, 'cause I think you all know how wonderful and special he was, I'm not going to bore you with that again, so I'm just gonna say this to you, Jim: 'I love you, mate. I'm never gonna forget you, I miss you so much, and you weren't just me uncle, you was like a brother to me.'" Suddenly choked, he whispers, "I miss you so much, mate. I love you so much. Every day." The applause is louder than ever.

Last comes Tommy, guitar in hand. "We're going to finish with some music. Jim loved this tune, written by me and a friend. I don't think there's anything left to say. I love you, Jim mate, for ever and ever."

The song is called "Sparkle", and has become a kind of anthem for the Jimmy Mizen Foundation, but then it was a complete surprise to Margaret: "I had no idea Tommy was going to sing, or that he'd written a song for Jimmy. I don't know how he got through it." His voice is clear and steady as he sings:

> Brother I feel weak,
> feels like hide and seek
> now you're gone.
> The directions you give
> are all that I live for but I'm lost.
>
> So come on and find me
> I know you're behind me,
> 'cause you sparkle.
>
> In a world that places
> blame on all the faces,
> where virtue means nothing
> and it's all about suffering,
> you made your difference here,
> the respect that you showed was so clear,
> sixteen years of you,
> showing honour beyond your youth.
>
> But your memory is deep inside
> and I'll never try to hide
> from your love.

So come on and find me,
I know you're behind me,
'cause you sparkle.

I'll never lose your sparkle,
I'll never lose your sparkle,
it brightened up the darkest day
and cheered up the saddest face,
no, I'll never look away,
no, I'll never look away
from your life.

Joanne, feeling unable to speak publicly of her deep love for Jimmy, has decided to keep her feelings private.

Last of all, with astonishing composure, Margaret speaks. She recalls Jimmy's birth on Cup Final Day, his brush with meningitis as a baby, his wonderful temperament all through his life. "I can't believe we're here now," she says. She raises many laughs with anecdotes of Jimmy's hypochondria, always wanting glasses (despite having perfect vision), or tooth braces, or crutches for the most minor injuries. At one point, she says to all her children, "I have to tell you how much I love you all. And Barry, I love you as well, so much." She speaks of Jimmy's faith, how he was happy to join in with her and Barry's daily readings and prayers, or carry his rosary. Last, she thanks Romek, a young friend of Samantha's, who also has Down's syndrome. His parents are Jimmy's godparents. "Romek has been our professional mourner," she laughs. "He has cried and cried with us. He shared every, every little bit of our pain. Thank you, Romek."

The final hymn is the well-known setting of the prayer of St Francis of Assisi, "Make Me a Channel of Your Peace". Last of all, Jimmy's coffin is carried by his brothers out of the church to Bob Marley's "Three Little Birds": *"Don't worry 'bout a thing, 'cause every little thing gonna be all right…"*

There had never been a funeral like it, with so many remarkable moments of beauty, pain, laughter, and hope. But the moment which everyone who remembers the funeral recalls is when the sixteen candles were brought forward by Jimmy's companions, lights guiding him home to an eternal rest, kindling a flame that would ignite the hearts and the imagination of thousands of people across the country and the world – but to do what? To try to fix what was broken? To fix Jimmy eternally in memory, for ever young, for ever innocent, a martyr for peace? Or was the song calling on Jimmy, on his memory, his inspiration, to fix us?

# 7

## Margaret's Letter

On 9 October 2008, five months after Jimmy's death, the *Daily Mirror* published an "open letter" written by Margaret to her son.

> Son, I sat down to write all the things I wish I'd said to you before you were taken. But I realized, luckily enough, that I'd said it all when you were here. I told you every day how much I loved you, how you made me proud, how special you are. So instead I thought I'd give you an update on everything that's happened since you died. I hope you're listening up there.
>
> It's difficult to say how our family has changed. Change is hard to see because it's locked inside people.
>
> We are coping by being together.
>
> Your brother Tommy has shelved his plans to go travelling next year because he wants to stay close to home. Danny wishes he was here all the time.
>
> Your brothers and sisters are putting on a brave face to help me and Dad, but they show their grieving in different ways.
>
> Harry and James miss playing the Wii with you each night in the games room. You always made a bet that whoever came last would have to make everyone a cup of tea, and it was always you who trooped out to the kettle at the end of another losing game.
>
> Samantha couldn't talk about you for a long time. Recently she was going through a list of people she

loved and she said your name, then quickly said sorry
because she was worried she'd upset me.

It's been really hard for Joanne. She had a special
relationship with you. She remembers the day you went
to the Noodle Bar and walked her to her car to ensure
she was safe, two weeks before you passed away.

She saw you walking away and thought you were so
tall and lovely, and wishes she'd told you how proud you
made her feel. You'd have given her that shy look and
big smile.

She's saved your MSN messages and wishes you
could both still chat.

Dad finds Saturdays in the shop painful – he was
used to you being there, misses your jokes, misses seeing
you out the back eating three sandwiches and a sausage
roll before you started work. Sometimes he feels you're
by his side when he walks to the car after closing. But
you are not there.

The other night Dad had a difficult evening because
he was missing you so much. He drove to the Aylesford
Priory and cried. He felt a bit better afterwards. I miss
you, you big lump. I wish you'd come into the kitchen
with a big smile on your face, plonk yourself on the
leather chair by the patio doors as you always did, with a
packet of crisps in one hand and a drink in the other.

Then you'd be at the fridge taking whatever you'd
find. It's odd to see ham or chunks of cheese still there
after a day or so – with you it always disappeared. I still
make too much dinner every night as I'm not used to
preparing less, especially when it's your favourite like
macaroni cheese or noodles.

Sometimes when I'm doing the washing-up the tears
come. If someone's here they'll come up and put their
arms around me. But I miss you coming up to me in the
morning and giving me a cuddle and saying, "See you

later baked potato" as you left for school each morning.
I just feel a real sadness since you died.

My faith keeps me going. You know how much I
like going to church and I couldn't miss Mass, it gets
me through the week. I miss seeing you at the back, at
6 ft 4 in head and shoulders above everyone else. When
tears come at night me and dad say a prayer together.
Lighting candles in church also helps me feel better.
Even the priests cried at your funeral.

As soon as you died I wanted your body blessed but
the priest wasn't allowed near because you were lying in
a crime scene. I felt I couldn't breathe until he did the
blessing later that evening when you were in a black bag
because then I knew for sure you were on your way to
heaven.

I have no doubt you are at peace and safe. But I
worry for your brothers and sisters. If they go out I wake
in the middle of the night and quietly check all their
bedrooms. I can't relax, it's a nightmare.

Not much has changed around the house, even
though it feels so different.

Looking after the garden was always your job, which
you did so well. Don't worry, we've been looking after it.
And, after almost five years of you nagging, we finally
put the water feature in. Tommy and your cousin James
built it in a shape of a "J" and I think you'd have loved it.

The other day I found your brace in the bathroom
cabinet – the brace you never wore. It gave me a real jolt.

I haven't left your room at it was, sorry son. Billy
came back from university in Oxford and has taken
up your half of the bedroom. We are a big family and
needed the space. Your things are all under the bed
and I haven't been able to move them yet. I hope you
don't mind if one day I go through your things and
share them among your friends. I think they'd all like a

memento of you but I'll never give away the safari hat you loved.

We don't need possessions to remember you – you are forever embedded into our hearts. We remember you saying, after your two young friends were killed in a car crash at New Year, that you just wanted to be remembered. If you can see how much has been done in your memory you'll be dancing in heaven.

We have boxes of cards and letters saying how sorry they are we've lost you. There are lovely letters from everyday people who didn't know you, and from very influential people like Cardinal Cormac Murphy O'Connor and Gordon Brown. You won't believe this, but we met the Prime Minister at 10 Downing Street and he seemed very caring.

Two apprenticeships at Lewisham College have been set up in your name. They said, after you did some work experience, that through you they saw the potential in youth and that your enthusiasm was infectious and rare in someone so young. There was a memorial dance at the rugby club, trees have been planted to commemorate you, and there are benches bearing your name at the cemetery and your school.

There's also a flower, called the Jimmy Mizen rose, and next year we'll get cuttings from it. It's a yellow rose – just the right colour to represent your youth, sunny personality and peace. I can see you now, thinking, "All this? For me'"

Of course, as a family we talk of you all the time and remember little stories. Like the time I took you to the doctor when you were a baby because you were just so good I thought there must be something wrong! Even as a toddler you threw no tantrums. Even when you caught meningitis you were placid. You were never miserable. I can't believe that you're gone.

There are a couple of things we did wish we asked you. We heard a rumour you might have had a girlfriend, and know you were due to meet a girl at the rugby club the night you died. Jimmy, was there someone special?

We also heard you might have liked the odd cigarette – was this true? Don't worry if it was. I know you were special, but you were also a very normal teenager.

You would talk and talk, and sometimes I'd think, "I wish you'd be quiet." Now I so miss the sound of your voice, our chats, hugging you and cuddling into that big chest of yours. It's so nice that you were never afraid of showing affection. I'm glad I always told you I loved you. But I just wish you were here so I could say, "Jimmy, make us a cuppa."

We miss you so much. Our lives go on but will never be the same. We have got to learn to cope and we will. Everything we do will be in your memory.

# 8

# The Trial

Jake Fahri gave himself up at Sutton Police Station on 13 May. He was charged with the unlawful killing of Jimmy Mizen at Sutton Magistrates' Court two days later. He spoke only to confirm his name and address, staring at the floor throughout. At one point he looked up to smile and wave to his girlfriend, who sat with her mother in the public gallery. His application for bail was refused and he was remanded in custody to be arraigned on a charge of murder at the Old Bailey on 21 August, at which point his trial date was set for 12 March 2009. This effectively sentenced Jimmy's family to live "in limbo" for almost a year. Everyone's plans were put on hold; for some, work proved impossible. The family are still paying off the financial costs of this period.

*Immediately after Jimmy's death we went out and put an extra £10,000 on our mortgage, to cover all the costs of the funeral and so forth. At the moment, we're not able to make any capital repayment; we're just paying the interest on the loan, and we're in a much weaker financial position. We owe more now than when we first took out the mortgage. There is a compensation process: the police give you a little booklet with contacts and information, and put you in touch with the Criminal Injuries Compensation Authority in Glasgow. There's a pay-out of about £11,000 for the victim's family but it's dependent on evidence; if it came out in court that the victim had started the fight, for example, you'd get nothing. So we didn't get the compensation until after the trial. The whole process was very expensive for us; during the trial, we had to put an extra £1,000 loan into the bank account just to cover train fares and lunches for the whole family, travelling back and forth to the Old Bailey every day. There was a big campaign about support for victims' families after Sarah Payne's murder, and the provisions are much better now.*

*Within a few days of Jimmy's death, Danny reopened the shop for us. He took that responsibility on himself, an amazing effort of will, which was absolutely wonderful. He was really suffering. He felt guilty because he'd been abroad – he felt he hadn't been there for his little brother "at the one time he really needed me". But he stepped in to keep the shop open and bring in some income for the family.*

*Harry had just started a job three days before, but he wasn't in any state to work after Jimmy's death. DCI Cliff Lyons wrote a lovely letter to Harry's employer explaining the situation and asking them to keep the job open, which they did, but of course they didn't pay him. Billy had just graduated from university and had intended to travel and look for work abroad in the hotel industry, but instead he came home to help look after the family. Tommy had quite a successful small business as a builder, but after a few months he lost the heart to work. He had plenty of work coming in, but he just couldn't do it. Eventually he went bankrupt. Bobby was working as assistant manager of a restaurant in Notting Hill – a tough, demanding job. They expected very high standards and you had to jump to deal with all the customers' demands and complaints. But when you're trying to deal with the fact that your younger brother's been murdered, the last thing you feel like doing is being nice to a lot of fussy customers in a posh restaurant. It was really hard for everyone. James was self-employed as a fitter for air-conditioning units, and he also had to take a lot of time off work.*

*At the end of June, one week after Jimmy's funeral, we all went on holiday to Spain. Essentially, it was Tommy's money that paid for it. He'd been paid for an exclusive interview by a Sunday newspaper, and he decided to spend the money on a holiday for everyone. We'd never been abroad all together as a family. We rented a lovely villa in Spain, with a swimming pool, and had the most wonderful time, but after just a few days I had a very bad accident. I'd got up in the night to go to the toilet and slipped on a tiled staircase and fallen head over heels all the way down. My knee had a huge gash in it and the bone was showing, but I'd also damaged my shoulder really badly and the bone was sticking out there as well. I thought I was dying! It was very scary. All I can remember is singing that Bob Marley song, "Don't worry 'bout a thing…" and drifting in and out of consciousness, and I could hear Joanne screaming, "She's dying! She's dying!" and Tommy was saying, "You're gonna be all right, Mum, you're amazing, you'll be OK!"*

*The ambulance staff couldn't speak English and we couldn't speak Spanish. The hospital staff stitched up my knee and put my arm in a sling, but they said I'd need an operation, which would be best carried out back in London. There was a Dutch doctor in the village where we were staying, and he bandaged me and strapped everything up properly, so I was able to stay for the rest of the holiday, with the help of painkillers. When we came home, I went straight to the hospital and they were really helpful. They operated the next day and inserted a pin to hold my shoulder together, which was removed eight months later, and in the end everything was fine. My care was excellent; we sometimes forget just how precious our National Health Service is.*

. . . . . . . . . . . . .

After the first flurry of police activity in the weeks following Jimmy's death, things quietened down over the summer, then in late October we were introduced to the Crown Prosecution Service (CPS) solicitor, and taken up to the Old Bailey and shown around by the Victim Support people, who explained the whole process. The CPS and the police were very helpful. But the defence team was getting busy as well at this point, contacting Jimmy's school and asking for his records (which were impeccable). They made a big fuss about his height, trying to build an argument by implication that he must have been a bully because he was so big.

We were told we couldn't talk to Harry or Tommy about what had happened, because they were both key witnesses, which was hard. And we were warned not to talk so much to the media, for fear of jeopardizing the trial, but we were trusting throughout that we'd say the right things, that God would give us the right words to say, that would not be a detriment to the trial, and that's how it turned out. The lawyers went through everything –all the TV interviews, newspaper articles –but couldn't find any compromising comments anywhere.

We were introduced to Clarence Mitchell through a friend of a friend, and he became our adviser during this period. After being a reporter for the BBC for many years, he'd left his job to become the press adviser and spokesman for the McCanns, following the abduction of their daughter Madeleine. Clarence was a great help and support to us throughout the whole period, guiding us through the storm of media interest, and during the trial he was there with us every day. He never asked for any payment, and we will always be deeply grateful *to him. He thought we already had a media adviser; apparently there was a lot of gossip circulating in media circles at that time over who was advising us, but there was no one. We were advising ourselves!*

. . . . . . . . . . . . .

In an interview recorded shortly before the trial, Danny speaks very frankly about his feelings:

"The bit I find hardest is that I'm the oldest brother, and of course when you grow up you always think you're going to be there for all your brothers, always look after them, no matter what happens. The one time he needed me I wasn't there for him.

"You know, my parents have been amazing: the comments they've made about this guy's parents, about feeling sorry for him and all that –I don't feel that way, OK? I feel a huge amount of anger. We ask, will this guy get a prison sentence? How long? We ask, what's right? What's justice? There is no justice. If he gets put away for ten years, it's ten years, you know; if he gets put away for fifteen, it's fifteen. It makes no difference. It doesn't bring my brother back.

"The way I feel? Totally honest –perhaps I shouldn't be saying this – give me him here. Give me just five minutes in a room with him here. It's completely wrong, but I don't care. 'Cause what goes through my mind the most is how scared my little brother must have been with this person attacking him. For no reason. For absolutely no reason. When Tommy found him in that cupboard with his hand on the door handle, 'cause he could feel it as he was trying to turn it, Jimmy didn't know what was going on, what was going to happen to him. Blood everywhere, which he could see, and how scared he must have been. Put him in a room with me, and I'd just love to make Jake feel as scared. It won't make any difference, it doesn't bring my brother back, wouldn't make me feel any better, but – and I know it's not the right thing to say – it's just the way I feel. I wish I could be as great as my mum and dad, and the rest of my siblings, but I've got this huge element of anger inside.

"If it all goes the way we hope it does, he'll be looking at life inside. But life isn't life. Life for Jake is going to be twelve years. The guy's nineteen. He comes out and in twelve years' time, he's thirty-one. He's my age. He's got his whole life ahead of him. He's getting out at the age I am right now, and he gets to live the rest of his life, while we – we don't get to see Jimmy again."

. . . . . . . . . . . .

*After Jimmy's death, an organization called the Nationwide Christian Trust, who produce films about people's stories of faith, commissioned a documentary about us, made by Humanity Productions. This production company then asked if they could work with us to make a film about the trial, but in the end, they couldn't secure a commission, so they decided not to proceed. However, the cinematographer, Benjamin Kempf, asked if he could film anyway.*

*We'd got to know him quite well and we all liked him, so we agreed. The result was a video diary entitled* The Hearing, *a powerful record of our family's experiences during the trial, which Benni subsequently entered in several film festivals. He said he thought he'd be making a film about anger, but what came out was a film about love. I have used this film, along with our recollections and newspaper articles, to construct the following account.*

Thursday 12 March 2009

*The trial begins today. I've barely slept a wink. I've spent most of the night praying. Now I'm up early, laying the breakfast table. Barry's already shaved and dressed in suit and tie, and is chatting with Samantha, reassuring her that we'll be back later. She's munching her toast and marmite and getting ready to go to her day centre.*

*One by one the rest of the family appear for breakfast, some half-dressed, some fully. There's a bit of chit-chat, but the atmosphere is pretty subdued. Barry's sister Dawn has turned up to mind the house while we're out. I'm so grateful to her, because I've been worrying about who's going to be there for Sam and George, and how we'll keep the house in order. I'm making a packed lunch for Sam, reassuring her as ever it's a cheese sandwich, packet of crisps, yoghurt, and a spoon, while Barry's pacing restlessly, hands in pockets, his eyes flitting across the family photographs on the kitchen dresser. "I don't want to feel Jimmy's been let down," he says to the camera. "I don't want to feel lies have prevailed. I want the truth to come out, and what the sentence will be, will be. It becomes irrelevant to us in the end because when it's done and over, I don't want to think about this person." His voice is calm. "If he gets ten years in prison or fifteen, whatever it is, I don't want to spend the next ten, fifteen years thinking about him." Barry is very much the strength of the family here, thinking above all about how to steer us through this harrowing time. "The pain I've seen in my children's eyes… I want to see that pain alleviated." I can see a tear in his eye. "And if for them it's a heavy prison sentence that alleviates the pain, then I'm happy with that. If, whatever the prison sentence is, any of them is still in pain, then I'm not happy with that. So I think there's really got to be a sense of justice on this."*

*For me, as long as Jake's character comes out, I can live with it. But if I'm honest, I don't know how I'm going to get through any of this. I feel bewildered. How can any of this be happening? Getting ready to go to the central criminal court in the land, the Old Bailey, to see a man stand trial for the murder of my son? We shouldn't be here, doing this, any of us. How on earth did this happen?*

. . . . . . . . . . . . .

*It's time to leave. Barry's saying goodbye to George, who's still in his pyjamas, Bobby's combing his hair in the mirror, last minute trips to the loo, coats and jackets on. George stands in the front drive, waving goodbye as we file out and set off for the station, following Jimmy's last route down onto Burnt Ash Hill. There's a reporter with a camera running alongside us, filming every step. Whether we like it or not, our private grief is now public property.*

*When we arrive at Cannon Street station, walking down the steps from the platform to the street, Joanne points out a couple standing on the pavement. "That's Jake's parents," she says. I've completely forgotten − of course, they live so near us, they had to be on the same train. They don't look up at us. I feel a wave of panic. I feel sick, tight-chested, dizzy. I'm also fascinated. How can two such ordinary-looking people have produced such a violent young man? Here we are, two mothers, with two lost sons, one killed by the other. Two mums now going into the same public courtroom to hear their sons' lives made public. What a sorry state of affairs.*

. . . . . . . . . . . . .

As we walk up to the Old Bailey, a huge crowd of photographers and TV crew is waiting for us. A young woman is doing a piece to camera for the BBC as we arrive: "It is extraordinary to think that a young man going into a baker's shop on a Saturday morning can end up dead, but that is exactly what happened. Nineteen-year-old Jake Fahri picked a fight with them, for no other apparent reason than he wanted to get to the cakes and they were in his way..."

At the corner of the Old Bailey, the police press officer Neil holds us back and gives us a few stage directions for the photographers: "Give them a group shot of the whole family, then Margaret and Barry step forward for a minute, and then you can just walk calmly into the court." This is what Clarence has told us already: if they want a picture, let them take one, then they'll leave you alone. If they want a story, give them a story, otherwise they'll make one up. Danny's muttering under his breath; he's fed up with photographers and journalists. Barry chuckles and winks at him and Danny grins in spite of himself.

As we troop forward towards the court entrance, I suddenly stop, paralysed. I feel sick and frightened; I want to run home and hide. I clutch Barry's hand, looking down, thankful that he's there beside me, with all my family. I recover, supported by Barry on one side and Billy on the other, and walk forward to face the music. Against the wall next to the entrance, a large crayon portrait of Jake Fahri has been placed, showing him in suit and tie in the dock next to a policeman, an artist's impression from his arraignment the previous August.

The young BBC correspondent's commentary continues: "The defendant Jake Fahri was seen running away with a smirk on his face. He handed himself in to the police three days later. He denies murder. He says he was simply defending himself..."

We greet Clarence outside the entrance to the court in a hail of flickering camera flashes and line up for the shots.

. . . . . . . . . . . .

The senior judge appointed for the trial is Mr Justice Calvert-Smith, former head of the CPS. They have dozens of possible candidates in court for the selection of the jury, so due to lack of space we've been asked, just for today, to sit with the press, in full view of the public gallery. We have to walk past Jake, sitting in the defendant's box, behind a thick glass panel, smartly dressed and showing no emotion at all. I look at him, and my first thought is, "You *silly, silly boy. What have you done? Not only have you ruined our family, but also your own – your mum's, your dad's, your sister's lives…"*

*Once we've sat down, I look up into the public gallery. There's a woman sitting with the Fahri family, an aunt maybe, looking down at us with an expression of pure hatred. I'm baffled – what have we done to her? I can still see her face. It was radiating absolute malice towards us. I thought, "It's our son who's dead, for goodness' sake." This is the only time we're in the full glare of the public gallery. The rest of the time we would be seated underneath it.*

*The court proceedings are so slow. It takes ages to establish the facts, but all the way through, you get so drawn into the whole process. You keep thinking, "It's like theatre; it is theatre," and you have to keep reminding yourself, "No, this is about my son. Everyone else here is at work; this is their job, but for us, this is our life." You're worrying all the time about the jury; there's one woman juror who keeps taking her coat off and putting it on again, and her eyes are everywhere, and I'm thinking, "She's not listening – wake up! Concentrate! Listen!" but of course you can't say anything. Then the defence start saying things, and you think, "That actually sounds quite plausible; the jury might believe it…" That's the cleverness of these barristers. They know what they're doing, sowing seeds in the jury's minds; if you want to study the art of public speaking, go to the Old Bailey. It's amazing – they sound so ordinary, using straightforward language, no complicated words, but it's loaded with subtle insinuations.*

. . . . . . . . . . . . .

*The first day in court is over. Thank goodness. The jury, mostly young women, has been sworn in. But now the defence have offered, unexpectedly, on the opening day, to plead guilty to manslaughter. Back home, we gather in the kitchen for an update. I'm making tea for everyone. Various newspapers carrying reports of the trial's first day are lying open on the table. Tommy interrupts my busyness, putting his arms around me, and gives me a big hug.*

*Barry sits down to speak to everyone gathered around the table. "OK then, basically what we've been told is that Jake Fahri is now going to put in a plea of manslaughter. Clarence believes the prosecution will dismiss it. We want a murder charge and a murder conviction. If they do downgrade it, we can't actually do much about it, although we will protest as much as we can."*

*Next to Barry, Danny's looking very fed up with the whole business —with the trial, the legal system, and most of all with being filmed in his own kitchen. Bobby asks, "If the prosecution say, 'We're not going for manslaughter, we're going for murder'and then he gets found not guilty, is that it?"*

*"Yes," says Barry. "No one's denying he killed Jimmy. So he's admitted to killing Jimmy, but so far all the way along he's been saying it's self-defence. If they can prove that, he walks out of the court." The boys are silent, contemplating this. "I don't know why they've changed it like this. Perhaps they realize that their excuse is so flimsy."*

*"From my point of view," I say, "I don't want anything less than a murder charge. I want justice for our darling Jimmy. It's got to be that. Nothing else is acceptable. Because it is murder."*

*I notice Danny gazing into space, as if he's miles away. "Danny-boy?"He throws open his hand in a gesture of don't-know and shakes his head. "It's cool. Whatever."The others are silent. He's struggling with too much pain to speak. "I haven't got anything to say. Whatever."*

. . . . . . . . . . . . .

Friday 13 March 2009

*As we're getting ready to leave for court, Samantha is watching* Friends *in the front room. In the kitchen, Dawn asks me, "Shall I just say the truth, then, when she asks where you all are?"*

*"She wouldn't understand," I say.*

*"Just say they're at work," says Bobby. "Then she'll ask you again," he says, grinning, "then she'll ask you again, and again, and again…"*

*I say goodbye to Sam on my way out.*

*"You come back?" she says.*

*"Yes, my darling, I'll be back later."*

. . . . . . . . . . . . .

*As we walk to the court, there are two girls skipping in front of us along the pavement. "Oh, isn't that sweet?" I say to Barry. One of the boys says, "No, Mum, that's his sister and his girlfriend; they're doing that to intimidate you." I can't believe it. Why would anyone want to hurt us any more? It's so unnecessary. In court, some of Jake's family are being confrontational up in the public gallery during the hearing, heckling, swearing, muttering rude comments. Some of our children are sitting next to them. We report this to the court officials and the family are warned. Walking back to the station each day, just a few yards away from them, then getting on the same train, is very difficult.*

. . . . . . . . . . . . .

*That evening, over the family dinner, Dawn is trying to piece together the correct version of events. "So he started smashing up the baker's because the boys wouldn't fight?"*

*"Not smashing up the baker's, no," I say, feeling a bit tired.*

*"Well, throwing things and everything," she says.*

*"No, no — attacking the boys with things."*

*Barry proceeds to give an account of the fight. I wonder whether we imagine those last few minutes of Jimmy's life the same way. We've never been allowed to discuss these events with Harry and Tommy, for fear of prejudicing their witness statements. The worst thing that's ever happened to our boys — and they're not allowed to tell us about it. I dread the thought of them having to make their statements in court, being cross-examined by that smart, sceptical defence barrister. Haven't they suffered enough?*

*"I don't think you can class him as a human being," interjects Andy, Joanne's boyfriend, "'cause he doesn't care about anyone but himself. And human beings do think about other people, and he doesn't. To not think about anyone else — that has got to be something to do with the upbringing." Andy has been very quiet till now. He seems genuinely astonished, uncomprehending — where could such behaviour have come from?*

*"See, I'm never quite sure about that," I say, "'cause my mum always said your nature's born in you."*

*"To a certain extent," he concedes, "but surely your parents teach you right from wrong?"*

*There's a single candle burning in the middle of the kitchen table, surrounded by parcelled-up food brought by friends and neighbours. Around its base, a string of heart-shaped silver beads has been strung; on its side, someone has written "Jim", underlined twice, followed by an exclamation mark. The "i" is dotted with a heart.*

. . . . . . . . . . . .

Monday 16 March 2009

*Harry and Tommy are due to give evidence today. They're leaving early for
the station, both looking very handsome in smart suits and ties, and we give
them a big hug on their way out. Barry's also dressed and shaved now, and he
speaks to the camera while he's tying his shoelaces. He seems brisk, practical,
no-nonsense: "If my children are content with the outcome, then I'm content
with the outcome. For me, it's as if this other person didn't even exist. This
just happened." He pauses, reflecting. "And it wasn't until I actually saw
him…that I had any sort of emotion or any feelings towards him at all. My
first reaction was that I felt like I wanted to throw up." Now he doesn't seem
so sure. Can we just ignore Jake? Pretend he doesn't exist? Whenever we see
a picture of Jimmy in the papers or on the news, there's always a picture of
Jake next to him. He's in our lives now, whether we like it or not. Isn't he?*

. . . . . . . . . . . .

*The film shows a series of fleeting sequences: all of us singing "Happy
Birthday" for Danny as he emerges into the kitchen, smiling ironically and
exchanging his special finger-to-finger touch with Samantha, a lifelong routine
between the two of them.*

*When we get to the Old Bailey, Colette McBeth is giving her daily
piece to camera, describing Tommy's ordeal in the bakery; cameramen and
photographers are rushing to snap each of us as we turn the corner into the Old
Bailey, and later Clarence is seen coordinating a shot of Harry and Tommy as
they leave the court after giving evidence.*

*They both deal with the cross-examination well. They answer the direct
questions, but there is nothing about feelings or emotions. Tommy says yes, he
went after Jake Fahri; yes, he went back and held Jimmy. It is the same with
Harry: "Did you fight with him?" "Yes, I fought with him"– that kind of thing.*

*Then Harry says to the jurors, "Jimmy was a bit shocked at the attitude
of the man. He basically said, 'Say please and I will move out of the way.'
Jake became very aggressive and stood right in Jimmy's face. I stepped in
because Jimmy is my brother, to stop any trouble. I said, 'There's no need for*

*any trouble.' He said he was going to wait for us outside the shop because he was going to give us a slap."* Then, later, he demonstrated to the jury how Jake had picked up the oven dish with both hands and hurled it at Jimmy from shoulder height. The defence counsel Sally O'Neill challenged him on this; she said Jake was trying to grapple the metal sign off Jimmy and had just picked up the dish with one hand and *"slung it"* in Jimmy's direction. Harry insisted she was wrong: *"It was thrown hard,"* he said. *"I didn't actually see it hit Jimmy. I just turned round and saw blood flying, lots of blood."*

After giving his evidence, he is so upset he has to leave the courtroom, so we follow him out. He breaks down in tears, and we hold him and hug him in the corridor. It is really painful.

Later, the video diary shows us all gathered in the bar just round the corner from the court. Danny's reassuring Tommy about his answers under cross-examination. *"The thing that's going to come across was that you were honest. You didn't lie."*

Tommy says, *"Basically, Zoe, the assistant prosecutor, was saying they can determine your character and say, well, this guy's obviously honest. He's not going to lie about anything. It will make us look bad if we try and make him look bad. And that's why they didn't bring it up about the things I shouted, you know, when I was chasing him. It's a good thing, but in a way I wanted to bring it up, you know?"* He grins. *"Stare him in the face and tell him that I wanted to effing kill him…"*

Danny cuts in, *"When they're saying things, you want to scream and shout because you know they're not true. When you've lived with someone all their life you know what they're like. We know Jimmy and we know Jimmy didn't react to anything. It was nothing to do with his size. Just because he was 6 foot-odd tall doesn't make him anything. That really frustrates me. Just because he was a big fella, just because there was a connection with rugby – as soon as they mentioned that, I wanted to give rugby up. I literally was going to be on the phone: 'I'm giving it up – I'm never playing it again in my life.' Because to have that connected, in some way affecting the outcome of the trial – I thought that was absolutely… disgusting."*

· · · · · · · · · · · ·

*Back home that evening, Harry and Tommy are chatting, sitting perched at either end of Tommy's bed in the room they share. Now they've both given their evidence, they're allowed – for the first time in nine months – to discuss what happened. Harry's a very quiet, gentle lad, but he's surprisingly animated here:* "To claim self-defence – who started the trouble? The two people, me and Jimmy, didn't ask for the fight. We said no. He left the shop then, came back in, then he hit Jimmy. Then we had to hit him back – that was self-defence from us. Couldn't not. Kicked him out of the shop, shut the doors. How many more times will he get told that we don't want the trouble? We shut the doors and still, somehow, in self-defence, he decides to break the glass door and fight his way back in. In self-defence, of course."

*Pinpointing the moment when he rang Tommy from the bakery, Harry says,* "There'd been no fighting at that point, had there? I'd rung you 'cause I could just tell this wasn't right. I wouldn't normally ring someone if I was in that sort of situation, because you wouldn't see the need. Butsomething just didn't feel right. And the fact of his aggression…"

*Tommy cuts in,* "When you rang me, I've always said that you were quite calm on the phone."

"Well, yeah, because nothing had happened at that point!" *Harry exclaims.* "He was outside but I still thought, I don't like the feel of it, so I thought I'd ring you up, get more people round, to scare him off… obviously didn't work."

"I mean, as I got to the crossing," *says Tommy,* "that's probably the exact moment where he hadthrown the dish. I was that close. I remember getting across and just seeing this guy run out."

"I don't know if he walked out and then ran," *says Harry.* "I only remember seeing him run from my part, then seeing you run after him. I was still behind the counter when I saw you run past. And then I came out…" *His face goes blank for a moment, staring, then he shakes his head and frowns.* "No. It is really blurry. I remember Linda, our neighbour, screaming at me – 'Is it Jimmy? Is it Jimmy? Harry, what's happened, is it Jimmy?' and she was crying as well. I was obviously crying. I didn't say much – just, 'Yeah'. Then Mum came running round, ran straight in the shop. Then two seconds later she came out and started saying how Jimmy was unconscious, and I wasn't expecting that! You can't expect that, can you? You can't think the worst." *He seems as bemused still as he was then.*

*Tommy agrees. "I kept going to Mum, 'He's fine, Jim's strong, he'll be fine, he'll pull through,' and yet I knew at the same time that he was dead. I was holding on to every last bit of hope I had, just hoping that he was still alive. But deep down, I knew. And when they came out and they took their gloves off and shook their heads…"*

*"That picture stuck in my head as well," says Harry. "Three or two of them, I think it was, came out, just took off their gloves and shook their heads. I don't think they even said anything."*

*"Everyone has guilt somewhere along the line, I think," says Tommy. "I do. All the time."*

*Perched at the other end of the bed, Harry pulls a face. "It's all hindsight. It's all ifs and buts. You can't think like that."*

*"No, definitely not. Although…" – Tommy's voice is very tentative, as if he almost feels foolish saying this – "I think I might start exercising a bit more."*

*Harry chuckles, recalling a comment in one of the many newspaper articles. "Well, yeah, I think, being called 'Overweight and cool' …"*

*"Exactly," says Tommy ruefully.*

*Harry giggles again, then corrects himself, "'Slightly overweight.' I got called 'the small one' about a million times. The small one! So I think I'm going to get myself stretched… get my body stretched."*

*"I keep wanting to time myself running round the corner," says Tommy. "I've never found out actually how long it took me to run round. I was crossing the road, and my phone was ringing. But then if I take into account looking at the phone, seeing who it is – couple of seconds – then answering it – like, another second, you know what I mean?"*

*"Reacting to it," Harry adds.*

*"Your reaction, y'know, the instant reaction – the answering and then the speaking must have taken…"*

*"Nine seconds we were on the phone."*

*"Nine seconds. You take all those things into account. It still must have taken a minute and a half to run round there."*

*If I'd run faster… if I'd answered the phone quicker… It's as if the central fact of their brother's death is so wrong, so unacceptable, that their minds are racing round and round trying to work out what went wrong – what went wrong and how can we fix it? We need something to fix. And with this goes guilt.*

*Harry's eyes lose focus, gazing back into memory.*

*Seeing and hearing my boys talking together like this, and knowing their pain, looking back, I find it hard to bear.*

• • • • • • • • • • • •

Tuesday 17 March 2009

*Toast and marmite for Sam's breakfast as usual. She's wearing a pretty patterned blouse and has brushed her hair beautifully. As always, she wants to check that everybody's coming back today.*

*"You'll come back," I say, smiling reassuringly.*

*"You?" says Sam.*

*"Yes, I'll come back."*

*Then she proceeds to name all the family and asks if they are coming back. Poor Sam: I wish I could do more, take all her anxieties away.*

*"Yeah, everyone, Sam," I smile.*

• • • • • • • • • • • •

*In some ways I don't really need to say goodbye to Jimmy, because I feel his presence with me all the time. Some days I get this overwhelming feeling I'm going to be sick, if I really think about it. I'm not sure I've even said goodbye. I don't think I've had a need to say goodbye, because I believe that I'm going to see Jimmy again. But this feeling persists, that "if we didn't do this, didn't do that…" Lots of people think, "If he'd stayed at home five more minutes…"*

*He was going to die at that moment. We had no say in it. It was just going to happen. And it did.*

• • • • • • • • • • • •

*Another train journey, another walk to the Old Bailey, in bright sunshine, and we are feeling a bit tired today, facing more photographs and another day in court. Then there is another journey home. A beautiful sunset lies across the rooftops of south London as the train heads east.*

*Back home, Joanne's reading* The Sun's *account of Tommy's evidence yesterday. Above a beautiful photo of Jimmy with his arm around Tommy's shoulders at a party, the headline reads, I HELD MY BROTHER AS HE BLED TO DEATH. Poor Tommy is strumming his guitar in the next room. In the front room, Barry's chatting with Billy and Danny. "What would you like to see as the outcome of this?" he asks.*

*Billy says, "If you're referring to the word 'justice', then it's impossible to get. We were asked the question today, what do we think justice is? To be honest, it's a bullshit word. It's a word made up by politicians to give some sort of...closure towards something. It doesn't really exist. Taking someone's life – how can you put some... real closure on it? You say, 'Oh, if you take someone's life, then this is what happens, this is the sentence you get.' Whether that be death in some countries – it's not justice."*

*Barry stirs. "I think the defence already know what they're going to say. She'll have a closing statement – 'As far as we're concerned, Jimmy Mizen punched our client, he pulled our client into the shop, blah, blah, blah... in the end our client was so scared he threw a dish –OK?' Whatever her story is. To get to that, she's dropping all these little hints, every time she gets up, to try and paint this picture. All those little seeds she's sown in the jurors' minds – and she'll put them together into a story. And it will be a believable story."*

*Danny casts his eyes to the ceiling.*

*"But you think, 'There's something wrong here,'" says Barry. "And you start to think, 'What is justice?' Justice is about the only thing that stops us all ripping each other apart, because there's that system and you live within that." Billy is listening, neither nodding nor interrupting. "Otherwise, you just go out there –"Oh, he killed him – we'll go round there and sort him out'– that sort of stuff. But we try and live within the rules, within the law. Without it you've got complete breakdown, anarchy, and all the rest of it. But by the same token it's got to be seen to be working in some degree. There's got to be some sort of consequences." He pauses. Then, nodding, he says softly, "But nothing brings Jim back. We know that."*

. . . . . . . . . . . . .

Wednesday 18 March 2009

*The video diary shows Danny sitting with Billy, James, and Harry, discussing the defence counsel's interpretation of the forensic evidence:*

"How do you get a piece of glass from a dish smashed onto a boy's face 2 metres and 13 centimetres into the air, stuck into the wall, in an upward direction? That's near-on impossible for a piece of glass without throwing it, without hitting it, with substantial force. I could do it – we could do a test now: break glass into a wall, OK, against an object, against this object here. We'll put this object in the middle, a metre away from the wall. We'll hit some sort of glass thing against it. See how hard it is, first and foremost, to break that glass. Then see how hard it is to get a piece to stick into the wall. And their argument is it wasn't done that hard. I can tell you now it is extremely hard. Get a bottle and try to smash it. Drop that glass, try and break it."

"They said they'd never seen it so deep as well," says Harry, pointing to his neck.

"As awful and graphic as this sounds," says Danny, "I'm not sure where the fatal cut was, but I think it was around here somewhere." He's pointing to the right side of his neck, beneath the chin. "OK, we'll say that area. Now it was 4 centimetres into Jim's neck. Now, get that finger and try and poke it into your neck 4 centimetres. I'm doing it now, maybe up to 2 centimetres' depth, and I'm using quite a lot of force, it's really difficult to get it any further. And there's a lot of give in the neck area. The skin is very elastic. She argued that a sharp piece of glass will cut through anything. Well, a sharp piece of glass would. But the Pyrex dish was whole when it actually hit."

"And the remainder of it has continued to travel…" says Billy.

"So it's not just a little bit of bad luck and it cut Jimmy," says Danny. "Oh, I can't talk about it. A lot of force was used. It's plain and simple. You don't even need a medical expert. You don't need an expert in glass, in materials, in what sort of glass. A lot of force was used."

. . . . . . . . . . . . .

A friend of Jake's, Damien Heaven, has been called by the prosecution as a witness. He changes his story halfway through, claiming that Jake broke the glass doors of the bakery kicking his way out, trying to escape from Jimmy and Harry's supposed attack, despite the fact that the broken glass was all inside the shop, not outside. After he'd finished, Crispin Aylett said to us, "Witnesses come in all shapes and sizes, but that's got to be one of the stupidest I've ever seen. He thinks he's done his friend a favour. He's actually just convicted *him." Much later, after the trial, a solicitor friend said, "I've no idea how the judge allowed Sally O'Neill to argue a plea of self-defence. It was ridiculous, with no basis and no witnesses."There were 120 police witness statements for the prosecution and a dozen live witnesses, all saying the same thing. At a certain point, the judge said, "We don't need to hear any more."'*

*The only witness the defence called, apart from Jake, was a glass specialist.*

. . . . . . . . . . . . .

Thursday 19 March 2009

*Early morning: George is watching cartoons in the front room, snuggled in a duvet on the sofa; in the kitchen, Barry's already dressed, preparing breakfast for Samantha. "Today is probably going to be quite distressing," he says to the camera. "We will hear the medical details of what happened. We've been advised it will be quite harrowing, but we just want to – in some way – share Jimmy's last moments. To get a real sense of what it must have been like. It's probably going to be very painful. I'm sure he was very frightened.But I think it's important just to go, and listen."*

. . . . . . . . . . . . .

*Today in court, they play the audio recording of Jake's original interview with the police. He says that he went into the bakery for a sandwich, then changed his mind and turned around to find Jimmy standing in his way.*

*"I've made a step and looked at him to say, you know, I'm trying to get past,"he says. "I didn't get no reaction, so I've brushed past him and he's obviously… he took offence to that, and he said, 'Don't touch me.'"He claims that Jimmy attacked him, and says he panicked when he thought he was losing his grip on the metal sign. Then he starts crying and says, "I can feel it coming out of my hands so I panicked. I looked to my left. There was a tray there. I picked it up and threw it. I didn't mean to hit him, I didn't. I just threw it. I thought he would put his hands up so he'd let go of the sign. All I wanted to do is, I didn't want him to hit me with the sign, so I picked up the dish. I didn't think it would smash and I threw it and it hit him. I didn't mean to hit him, didn't want to hurt him, didn't want to. I might have been lippy at the start, you know, but I didn't mean it to happen."*

He says he ran off when Jimmy let go of the sign, and that he'd only learned of Jimmy's death when his mother Shirley rang him, unaware of his involvement, to tell him what had happened in the local bakery. You can hear his voice cracking as he says, "Someone has died because of me. I didn't mean it. I didn't mean to kill him. I've got a mum and dad. I know he has a mum and dad. I'm sorry. I was lippy at the start, maybe I was aggressive, but I didn't mean that to happen. I didn't want to cause him harm."

The video diary shows Danny and Billy sitting with their heads in their hands, almost speechless, in the nearby pub. I can't bear to see them suffering so much. Billy looks up. He looks like he's been crying. He looks bewildered. He's never normally lost for words.

"The only reason he's crying," says Danny, "is that he knows he's gone too far, finally – out of all his life, out of all the stuff he's committed. So now he cries. It's for no other reason. He knows he's gone too far. So now he's crying out of emotion. It's not out of… that he thinks… he was the victim or anything like that. But it comes across as if he's, like, the victim. He wasn't a bloody victim…" He bursts into a torrent of swearing. "His family are smirking all the time – they all smile, happy as Larry… we're the ones that have had the loss! We're the ones that have to deal with this shit every day and we feel like we're guilty!" He mimics Jake's interview tape, "It's the bakery I used every day for God knows… all the time… blah, blah, blah… he started crying his eyes out in the interview and saying that… basically it was Jimmy and Harry, they were raining blows down on him… He was just bawling his eyes out…"

Harry is eating a sandwich. He looks so sad, completely blank, not angry, not grieving, just lost. I want to take him in my arms and make everything better.

. . . . . . . . . . . . .

Back home, Danny's still raging against the defence counsel's version of events: "The bigger guy was aggressive and whatever else, the bigger guy said that. And if you're listening independently, you might think, 'It does sound feasible…' The problem is, we have to keep defending our brother who shouldn't need to be defended… It almost puts doubt in your head. Suddenly you start thinking, 'Perhaps I didn't know him that well. Perhaps he could have done that.'"

*Billy says, "If by any chance — and it's always in the back of your head — this guy might get off, that's a scary thing. But if he's proved innocent, that means that what they're saying about Jimmy is, in the eyes of the court — the law — true. The bad things they're saying about him. That's a real scary thought."*

*"If Jimmy was such an aggressor," says Danny, "so wanted a fight, so up for it, OK — why didn't Jimmy step outside? Why didn't Jimmy confront him? And the worst bit is, if Jimmy had started it, he would have gone outside and he'd probably still be here today. It would've been a quick fight — over and done with — plain and simple. "Let them put his mum into the dock. Ask her, when she phoned him up to tell him what had happened, not realizing it was her son — how was his reaction? Any time Mum's phoned me and there's been a problem, she's known it through the tone of my voice. If I've ever had a problem, I'd probably try and hide it, but as a mum, you just know. "I hope, to the very day he dies, to the very day, he never forgets Jimmy's face, to the very day, everywhere he goes — morning, noon, and night — the thought in his head… is Jimmy. Jimmy with that smile."*

*In the next room, Barry's put on some old family videos of Jimmy as a young lad, painting a garden chair bright red while I'm sanding down another in the background, Jimmy trampolining with Tommy and George, Jimmy building a huge sandcastle on the beach with George in the middle. Jimmy's bright smile and his beautiful, dark eyes and his laughter speak the truth of his character. Barry's crying.*

. . . . . . . . . . . . .

Friday 20 March 2009

*A short day in court. We've returned home for a late lunch and we're sitting around the kitchen table discussing the wording of our "impact statement". Barry's scribbling a couple of final phrases, then he "ting-tings" his pen against a glass to call for order, chuckling at the pretend-formality.*

*"OK, everyone?" he says, "All right, here it is:"*

As the parents of Jimmy Mizen, and on behalf of
our family, we understand the purpose of the impact
statement is to let the court have an idea of the effect

his unlawful killing has had on his family and not, in any way, to be an influence on any sentence that may be imposed. We think that the suffering of most of us is something we don't want added to the court records and only wish to talk about the effects on our daughter Samantha, who is twenty-two, and our youngest son George, who is nine. We would also like to speak about the character of Jimmy as, so far, no information about him has been heard apart from "He came from a loving family." It's been painful to hear him described as a "huge young man", an insinuation that he was of an aggressive disposition, as if your height in any way adversely reflects your character.

Since Jimmy's death, our youngest son George, 9, has slept on the floor of our bedroom. He cannot face sleeping in his own room, and asks for the windows to be shut and the curtains drawn. We hope, with love and care, we can help him deal with this fear. Our daughter Samantha, 22, has Down's syndrome. We love her dearly and have always seen her as a special gift. Samantha has very poor communication skills and does not say much at all. Every time either we go out anywhere or someone takes her out, her response is always the same since Jimmy died. She says, as a question, "Come back?" either to us or about herself. She will also run through the names of all her siblings with the same two words, "Come back? Come back?" Obviously this is in response to the fact that Jimmy went out and didn't come back. We continually reassure her and hope in time she will become less anxious.

We now come to our dear son Jimmy. He was a fine young man and a pleasure to be with. He was described by his teachers as having a gentle nature and being a joy to teach. Our treasured memories are of someone with a non-judgmental character, who would relate to anyone

and get along with anyone of any age or background.
He was polite and courteous and always seemed to be
happy. He enjoyed life. His loss is immense not only to
us but to all his friends. Jimmy was the shining star in
our family and will always be remembered with a smile.
We are so proud to have been his parents. God bless
you, Jimmy.

*I'm utterly exhausted. I've hardly slept during the trial. Since Jimmy's death,
a full night's sleep is a rarity for me. I often get up in the night and roam the
house, checking my adult children's bedrooms in the small hours to make sure
they've all come home.*

· · · · · · · · · · · ·

Monday 23 March 2009

*Jake took the stand today. He was clean-cut, well-dressed, controlled his anger,
spoke very clearly, and there was no great emotional display, which I'd been
expecting. When he was asked about mugging Harry, years back, he said, in a
very innocent tone, "It was just for a packet of sweets!" When Crispin Aylett
was questioning him, Jake wouldn't stop talking. Having watched too many
film courtroom dramas, I think we were waiting for him to lose his composure,
to start ranting and showing the court what an angry person he is, but it didn't
happen. Nor did he start crying and pleading how sorry he was. He just
stuck to the same story he had concocted, to try, in whatever way possible, to
get away with what he had done. However, he did start talking unprompted:
perhaps he thought he could influence the jury, I don't know, but he went on
and on and, after a while, Crispin just sat down. Eventually, perhaps to stop
him incriminating himself, one of the defence barristers got up and said, "I
think you'll find my learned friend has finished."*

· · · · · · · · · · · ·

*As we were leaving the court, the young BBC correspondent was reporting the
day's evidence to the camera: "Fahri today said he never meant to kill Jimmy
and was acting out of self-defence. He said, 'I grabbed the dish by its side. I*

*didn't think it would hit him. I just flung it. It never entered my mind it might break.' Fahri did admit, however, that he knew he'd hurt Jimmy. He said, 'I saw it hit his face round the jaw area. I saw the glass break, and I saw a bit of red. At that point I ran off.' But the prosecution ridiculed Fahri's account. Crispin Aylett QC said Fahri had been full of fury that day because he'd been humiliated, laughed at, and left impotent with rage. It was, he said, a stupid argument about loss of face, and Fahri had come out on top. During Fahri's account, Jimmy's mother left the court, too upset to listen. The family went home tonight knowing his evidence is now over..."*

. . . . . . . . . . . .

Tuesday 24 March 2009

*The next morning, I'm discussing Jake's performance on the witness stand with several of the boys.*

*"I thought he'd have a reaction," says Danny, "sort of lose his temper... I just wanted to see a sign of emotion, and there wasn't."*

*A lot of the time yesterday, Jake was huffing and puffing in court, sighing, yawning, tutting, and leaning his head on his hand as if he was bored. There was no sign of any remorse at all.*

*"After seeing him on the stand," says Billy, "you realize – he doesn't feel anything, anything whatsoever. It tells you something about him, doesn't it – that he's deluded."*

*I'm so fed up with all this. "Jake's character is well known in our neighbourhood," I say. "With Jimmy, we're having to justify a boy who's of immaculate character – absolutely immaculate character – and so's Harry."*

*"The problem is, you don't know what the jury think," says Danny. "I was just hoping for one little show of remorse, one little show of 'I really mucked up here and take responsibility.' He's actually acted like a kid who's got into trouble and is thinking of every excuse possible how to get out of it. And he's almost got it set in his mind, 'No, this is definitely what happened. No, it was definitely this way.' We all know it's not. And the problem is, he's got it like that and he's seen it like that and it's all clear-cut to him, so the story he's fabricated sounds true. For his side to be true, every other single statement – taken from everybody else – must be wrong."*

*I'm lying back exhausted in an armchair. "I know, with every breath in my body, that Harry and Jimmy had no aggression in them," I say. "And we're sitting here justifying something we don't need to."*

*"I don't actually see him getting convicted of murder," says Danny. "I don't see it happening. And that feels devastating."*

*Barry's joined us. "Crispin Aylett said today that it's unusual for a jury to convict a nineteen-year-old of murder," he says.*

*I'm sick of trying to justify things. Jimmy was a good boy.*

. . . . . . . . . . . . .

Wednesday 25 March 2009

*I feel so weary. When the jury delivers its verdict, maybe today or tomorrow, it means we can try to move forward, instead of having this awful weight hanging on our shoulders. Which is what it's been for the last ten and a half months.*

*It was nice going to church last night, though, because I felt I was really struggling yesterday. I went to church and felt a real uplifting, to get me through today. Because when they give the verdict today, or tomorrow, I'm not sure if I'll have my hands over my ears or not.*

*But what I find difficult is that, for so many people around the court, this is just a job. You're playing with people's lives, but it's just a job. There's no emotion from anyone.*

. . . . . . . . . . . . .

*After today's hearing, Clarence travels back on the train to Lee with us. He's lined up a number of television interviews this afternoon. He says he's got something like twenty possible interviews lined up, if we want to do them. I can't understand why anyone would be so interested in us.*

*"You've got a strong message you want to convey," he says. "You've taken that decision to go public with it. It's in Jimmy's memory and it's in your interest to use this opportunity now, because this attention won't be there for that much longer, let's face it. But it's legitimate; you're not hogging the limelight. You're not going out seeking it; they've all come to me. I'm just refereeing them, basically."*

· · · · · · · · · · · ·

*Back home, the house is beginning to fill up with reporters, camera crews, photographers. Clarence has an impressive line-up: BBC national television news, Sky News, Channel 5, BBC London and London Tonight, photographers from the* Evening Standard *and* The Times. *The young woman who's been covering the case for the BBC arrives and introduces herself as Colette McBeth. I say that I remember her sitting quite close to me in court and getting quite upset at one point.*

*"Oh, I'm sorry!" she laughs. "Yes, yes, I did. I've got two little boys, you know, and I just found it really… Don't tell anyone, though: I might lose my job!"*

· · · · · · · · · · · ·

*The cameras are rolling now, and Colette's interviewing us in the garden. "I think what's surprised a lot of people," she says, "is that you don't seem to be angry or bitter. Does that still stand?"*

*"The words just came out of my mouth," I say. "I don't remember thinking, 'I'm not angry', but for some reason I must have said it. But d'you know what, it's anger that killed Jimmy, and I could be angry now, and what's going to happen? It's going to make me more difficult to live with for my family. They need me."*

· · · · · · · · · · · ·

Thursday 26 March 2009

*Sally O'Neill made her closing statement for the defence today:*

*"No one is suggesting that Jake Fahri intended to kill Jimmy Mizen. It is the prosecution's suggestion that he intended to cause really serious harm. In reality neither is remotely likely. Jake Fahri had no more intention of causing really serious harm than Jimmy Mizen had of causing really serious harm to Jake Fahri when he pushed him into that glass display case…*

*"Whatever you may think of Jake Fahri's behaviour during these few minutes, in our submission the only piece of evidence pointing to Jake Fahri intending to cause serious harm is the fact that the dish broke and, as a result*

*of breaking, the shard went into Jimmy's neck with such tragic consequences. Both of those consequences were entirely unexpected and certainly unintended. No one would have expected that dish to have broken."*

*Closing the case for the prosecution, Crispin Aylett told the jurors they must decide two questions: first, whether Jake was acting in self-defence, and second, whether he intended to cause serious harm to Jimmy. "I suggest that Mr Fahri was not defending himself and that he was trying to cause serious harm," he said. "If you agree with me, then this must qualify as murder. If you throw a glass at someone's head, intending to cause serious harm, and the glass causes serious injury, then you can't really complain if you are convicted of murder. It will give you no pleasure to convict a person of murder – especially a nineteen-year-old – but if you decide the evidence proves he did murder Jimmy, then it is your duty to do just that."*

# 9

# The Sentence

Friday 27 March 2009

*I have mixed emotions about Jake's family because, at the end of the day, they might be good people. I don't know. Who am I to judge and say? I just don't know. So I don't feel I have any right to feel anything other than sorry for them.*

. . . . . . . . . . . .

*The jury retired at lunchtime yesterday. We went out, and the boys went off to the pub somewhere. Crispin told us they'd asked for a few exhibits, which he said was promising. They wanted to see the shop sign which Jake had used as a weapon, and to engage in a bit of role-play or re-enactment, to see how it was used. It feels like a million years. Waiting around at the Old Bailey in the family room, with all my children, including George, who's been allowed to come in specially for today, and some of Jimmy's friends. Sixteen of us. The Victim Support volunteers have kindly provided a new tin of biscuits, which disappears in five minutes.*

*All of a sudden it's announced over a loudspeaker: the jury have made their decision and the court will reconvene in fifteen minutes. It is the most terrible feeling.*

*So we go back in. We're sitting very close to Jake, just a couple of yards away. He's behind a glass screen. A couple of burly City of London policemen are standing between us and Jake. The foreman of the jury is a balding, tubby gentleman of Middle Eastern appearance. He stands up. The judge asks him, "How do you find the accused, guilty or not guilty on the charge of murder?" I have my hands over my ears. My heart's pounding. I feel sick. But I still hear him say, "Guilty." There's a sort of subdued gasp of "Yes!" from all our family and our group, and then everybody's weeping and hugging each other. No joy. No triumph. Just relief.*

*Crispin Aylett reads out our impact statement. Jake is overheard in the dock, saying, "I don't wanna listen to this shit." How can he be so stupid? To behave like this immediately before the judge passes sentence? The judge thanks us for the clear and moderate wording of the impact statement, and then quietly studies his notes while we wait in silence. After fifteen minutes, he addresses Jake.*

*"You had two opportunities to reflect," he says. "You went back, determined to cause very serious injuries if you could, to Jimmy Mizen, who you felt had disrespected you. In fact, you carried out your intention so successfully that you killed him, depriving a loving family of a son and brother. A trivial incident, brought about by the defendant's rudeness, escalated into something horrific. The defendant reached for any and every available weapon with which to attack the Mizen brothers. The whole incident lasted no more than three minutes – three minutes of absolute madness on the part of this defendant. A trivial incident over absolutely nothing in a high-street bakery ended three minutes later with the death of a blameless young man. However, the court accepts that you did not intend to kill your victim and that you are a very young man."*

*Jake is sentenced to life imprisonment, with a minimum term of fourteen years. As they take him away to the cells, he calls out to his mother, who's weeping in the gallery, "I will be all right, mum. I'll be all right."*

. . . . . . . . . . . .

*As we come out of the court into the street, Clarence is marshalling a huge throng of reporters and cameramen. Barry and I walk out with George between us into a barrage of microphones and cameras flashing and clicking. George looks slightly bewildered, but also faintly amused, as if he's watching some strange animals in a zoo. We form a group for the cameras, with Cliff Lyons and our Family Liaison Officer Kerry. Cliff steps forward.*

*"Good afternoon. My name is DCI Cliff Lyons. I've been the officer leading the investigation into this very sad and sorry tale." He's standing square on to the cameras, feet planted wide, hands behind his back. George has taken up a similar stance next to him, with his hands clasped formally across his tummy. He has a great sense of occasion. Maybe it's his altar-boy training.*

"Much has been made of what Jake Fahri has said about this incident and the fact that he apologized to Jimmy's parents. That is nonsense, and the jury have rightly delivered a unanimous verdict of guilty in this case. Jimmy Mizen was indeed an immaculate and decent young man. That never really came out during this trial. He's a credit to himself and his parents."

Harry's coming out now, looking haunted, ashen, wiping his eyes, supported by Joanne. The rest of the family are following him and form a group behind us. Cliff continues, "I've the utmost admiration for Barry and Margaret Mizen, who've shown tremendous dignity and grace during this whole process, and even found it in their heart during this awful incident to have empathy for Jake Fahri's parents. What fantastic people.

"Jimmy Mizen is an individual that... I think we'd all aspire to have a son like him. Jake Fahri is from an entirely different world, a yob, that part of society that we hold apart. He was extremely violent, and the jury has returned a just verdict, and I congratulate them on listening attentively and coming to the right verdict." He thanks the witnesses, "who gave statements to the police in their numbers and made the difference", then thanks the police teams, the CPS, and the prosecution barristers, and then turns to face us. "And finally, I'd just like to pay further respect to Jimmy's parents," he says. "It's been a pleasure to serve you. You are fantastic people. I now hope this gives you some... some way of trying to come to terms with this awful incident. Jimmy Mizen, rest in peace." He seems genuinely moved. Barry thanks him quietly, patting him on the arm.

We haven't prepared any speech, but it seems right to say something. Barry steps forward.

"I'm just going to say a couple of things," he says. "I want to say a few thank-yous, so please bear with us. I want to say thank you to the people of this country, who've sent messages of love and support throughout this. It's been a great help to us; thank you to all of them. I want to thank the people in our local community for the very practical ways in which they've been supporting us through this trial as well. I actually want to say thank you to the police, the officers of the Met police that have been with us. I want to say thank you to DCI Cliff Lyons, thank you to our Family Liaison Officer Kerry Ash, thank you to two other ones in the immediate team, Detective Sergeant Richie Reynolds and Detective Constable Karen Miller. Their professionalism, *their compassion for us, their dedication and hard work is to be admired and appreciated. I want to say thank you also to Clarence Mitchell for his support throughout this; it has helped greatly. I want to say thank you, myself and Margaret, to our children. They have shown dignity and restraint throughout this. Well done.*

*"I want to thank God for Jimmy... thank God for his life. It was a pleasure and a privilege to have been his parents. We miss him dearly. D'you know, this country has been known for many hundreds of years — and it stands apart from most other countries in the world — as a country of civility, a country of fair play, fairness, and a country of safety, and we are rapidly losing that. We're becoming a country of anger, of selfishness, and of fear, and it doesn't have to be like this, and let's together try and stop it. Thank you."*

*He steps back and, without thinking, I move forward to speak. "I thought about not saying anything," I say, "but I need to say a few thank-yous as well, really. Going through this, there's been so much going on, but the people of our parish, our friends, have provided us with a meal every evening, so we could go home, after this hard day, and there'd be a meal on our table, and also friends of ours have opened their houses up every evening for people to come together to pray for our family. I think it's amazing, and I just want to say a special thank you to them. And also to my sister-in-law, who's kept my house going; she's done my washing, made our beds, looked after Samantha and George most days. And I want to say thank you to you, the press, because I feel that some of you felt our pain, and thank you very much. Thank you."*

*I smile and turn away, and our family move away down the street, arms around each other.*

. . . . . . . . . . . . .

*Some people say fourteen years isn't enough. I'm not in the least bit interested in the sentence. All we wanted was the truth. People expect you to be joyous. I don't feel that either. It was always about the truth. We've been praying every night during the trial, along with our friends, not for a guilty verdict, but for strength for all the family and for the truth to come out. Even on the way to court each day we've been praying, walking along to the Old Bailey, holding hands, trying to hear each other over the sound of the traffic.*

*When I got home today, I just cried and cried and cried, like I've never cried before. Everything came out: relief that the truth had been upheld, but also my sadness and overwhelming weariness.*

*The realization that Jimmy is actually dead… Yes, you've seen the body and had the funeral, but now, with the trial over and the truth known, there's a new realization of what's happened. It's like Barry says: slowly, one by one, all these strings connecting him with Jimmy are being cut. Up till the trial you're in limbo, but the sentencing was another milestone, another marker on the path to "closure". Barry says he lives in fear of all the strings being cut and losing his connection to Jimmy altogether, of seeing him slip away into memory. As each day passes, do we get a day further from Jimmy, or a day closer?*

. . . . . . . . . . . . .

*The other day, I drove past Jake's house, thinking he's still alive somewhere, and Jimmy's not… sometimes it feels like the trial's still going on.*

*I used to drive past their house a lot. I don't any more, but up until a couple of years after the trial, I was doing it every other day. All I see is a house just like ours. I never saw any of the family, and the blinds were always shut. But I always wanted to look at them and maybe try to understand why their son turned into the angry young man he is.*

*I do wonder in my heart how they're feeling and I sometimes think I'd love to really know. I'd love to talk to them. And, in a way, I'd like to talk to Jake. I'd like to ask him what made him so angry, what made him angry with life. I don't have the hate for him that I should as a mother. I should be gritting my teeth and really hating him, but somehow I can't.*

*One of the teachers from his primary school, Tom Crispin, was interviewed for the TES newspaper shortly after the trial: "I remember Jake Fahri well," he said. "When people have asked me about him, I have recalled the comment of a colleague in the staffroom all those years ago: 'If you'd held him under water for ten minutes, he'd still have come up smiling.' Such was the arrogance of the boy that no matter what sanction was imposed against him, it would have little or no effect." (15 May 2009)*

*We feel that there are young people growing up in the wrong way, and we as a society are allowing them to become the thugs in our communities. Why are we surprised? When we go into prisons, we find they're full of people who've made bad decisions, not bad people. Neville Lawrence himself, the father of Stephen Lawrence, when Jon Snow asked him on Channel 4, "Do you blame the boy?" said, "No. I blame the parents." He blamed the culture that they grew up in. Now Jake doesn't come from the usual obviously deprived family background of many prisoners – absent father, alcoholic or drug-addicted mother, etc. – but appears to have a stable family background. I often wonder what his upbringing was like.*

*What did Jake learn? What was his acceptable behaviour? How was he encouraged? We've never taught our sons to get the first kick in, or to retaliate. Should we have done? Would Jimmy still be alive if we had? These are the questions that drive us to focus on this idea of early intervention –it's about the formation of people. And if you're being formed in a bad way at home, and it's apparent at school (and you talk to schoolteachers and they say they can always pick out the kids who are going to go off the rails),what do we do as a society? What is our responsibility? Do we let it just carry on? We'll tell you off, we'll give you a little fine and a slap on the wrist, and then, now you've killed someone, we'll lock you up for twenty years. Whose responsibility is it?*

*What is forgiveness? For Barry, it means he's got no desire to do to Jake what Jake did to Jimmy. No desire to seek retribution, vengeance for what he did. For him, that's forgiveness. It's not excusing what Jake has done –it's saying, I do not wish to do the same back to you. It doesn't go any further than this. For me, I believe God freed me from being consumed with anger and hatred, and instead gave me a deep empathy.*

. . . . . . . . . . . . .

*Shortly after Jake Fahri gave himself up to the police, Erwin James, a former double murderer who spent over twenty years in prison, wrote an article for* The Guardian *about what Jimmy's murderer might expect inside:*

> Life in prison for the perpetrator of this crime… is going to be demanding. He would begin his sentence in a Young Offenders' Institution, where the dynamics of the prisoner hierarchy are not so different to those in an adult prison. On the landings he would be notorious, a "celebrity con". There would be no hiding place wherever he went. Other

prisoners would know long before he arrived in their jail that he was coming. And once on the wing, they would whisper and point.

Because Jimmy Mizen was under 18, his killer would be a "schedule one"offender – officialese for a child killer. Though there seem to be no redeeming features about what he did, he is not a child killer in the strictest prison sense, so his fellow prisoners may not hold that particular aspect of his crime against him. Nevertheless, he is not a bank robber, or a major drug baron. So if he does not give the impression quickly that he is to be feared, he would be targeted.

To protect himself he could either express a fierce willingness to again use violence and "front"any potential antagonists at the earliest opportunity, regardless of the consequences. Or he could "go on the numbers"(Rule 43: segregation for own protection) –and ask to be isolated from the main prisoner population in a VPU, Vulnerable Prisoner Unit.

The only hope he would have of achieving anything good with his prison time, however, is if he chose to do neither.

If he managed stay on the landings and stand his ground against those who might want to make his life more difficult, without resorting to threats or violence, then he might have a chance. For all the limitations that prison life provides, there are facilities and opportunities that can help to bring meaning to a wasted life. So much would depend on the choices he would make.

· · · · · · · · · · · ·

*In November 2009, Jake was stabbed four times in the back with a pair of tweezers sharpened into a "shank"– an improvised knife – by Sean Mercer, an eighteen-year-old inmate serving a life sentence for the murder of eleven-year-old Rhys Jones in 2007. He was pinned down by another prisoner while Mercer stabbed him in the exercise yard at Moorland Young Offender Institution in Doncaster. Paramedics administered emergency care to save his life and he was rushed to hospital, where surgeons succeeded in stabilizing his condition. A prison officer said the blade ricocheted off Jake's spine and nearly killed him. "Fahri was just a few millimetres away from being paralysed by one of the stab wounds. He was in a terrible state, moaning with pain and covered in blood. The most likely motive was to give Mercer jail credibility and to prove he is the most vicious inmate —and therefore top dog. Astonishingly, he is looked up to by some young thugs serving time with him."*

*Raphael Rowe, another ex-offender who's now an investigative journalist for the BBC, got in touch with us after this and wanted to interview the two mums, me and Mrs Fahri, for a* Panorama *programme. Our children weren't too happy about this but said yes, OK, so I agreed and initially Mrs Fahri said yes, but then Jake was attacked again and she pulled out. She was worried that if she did anything to draw further attention to Jake, it might make things worse for him in prison. So there's a sad story in there somewhere, and a mother who undoubtedly loves her son.*

· · · · · · · · · · · ·

*At the end of his article, Erwin James concludes,*

> As he moved through the system, transferring to the high security estate when he reached 21, he would have to try to come to terms with his actions, as well as surviving. There are people who work in our prisons who would endeavour to help him, but his crime would be a load that only he could bear. He would never be able to make up for what he had taken away. But he could make the effort to find the courage to use his prison time well and to find a better way to live than he did before. He would owe that much at least to Jimmy Mizen and his family.

· · · · · · · · · · · ·

The day the trial ended, Danny was interviewed in our kitchen by Kay Burley, for Sky News. "I've tried to hate this person," he says, "but I can't."

# 10

# A Legacy of Peace

This chapter was originally adapted by Leah Kreitzman from interviews with Barry, as the opening chapter of a pamphlet entitled 'Punishment and Reform:How our justice system can help cut crime', commissioned for the Fabian Society by the Rt Hon Sadiq Khan MP, Member of Parliament for Tooting, Shadow Lord Chancellor and Shadow Secretary of State for Justice since October 2010.

It is impossible for a parent to prepare for the emotion you feel when you lose a child. There is no single right way to deal with the grief. It can be all-consuming and, after more than three years, it is still gut-wrenching in a way that is at times physically painful. Just as each child that has been lost to violence on our streets is unique, so is the way grief is felt by the family members they leave behind. No one hands you a manual of how to cope and everyone's experience is different. When our family lost our beloved son Jimmy, it changed our lives irrevocably.

All our relationships have changed to some degree as we've each tried to adjust. But we know we have to support each other or we would all individually fall apart. We are determined not to let what happened to Jimmy do any more damage to our family and that a positive impact on the lives of other young people would be the legacy of our son's death. We decided that if we could channel our energies into assisting young people in our community we could help to make the sentiment many bereaved families share into a reality – that we will not be beaten by what happened and something good must come from it.

We were exposed to the machinery of our criminal justice system – an experience that thankfully very few families will ever have to bear. Rightly, due process has to be followed for both the defendant and the victim, so the process can be long, complicated for people without a legal background and very difficult. The perpetrator of Jimmy's murder, another local teenager with a history of bullying and destructive behaviour, was convicted and given a life sentence, with a minimum tariff of 14 years. For us, getting justice for Jimmy was not just about punishment for his killer, it was about finding and exposing the truth of what happened to our son.

In the immediate aftermath of Jimmy's death we needed answers about what had happened and how, and about who was responsible and what would happen to them. These were questions for the authorities – for the police, the lawyers, and the courts. But we soon began asking deeper questions that no Government or public body could answer alone: what has gone so wrong that young people are killing each other on our streets? What can we do to ensure young people don't resort to violence against each other? What sort of values should govern our society and how do we ensure they are instilled in all our young people? How can we stop a child born today from becoming a violent adult? Working towards finding answers to these questions is what we've been trying to do since Jimmy's death.

Not long after Jimmy died, my wife Margaret and I were invited to a local school by the chaplain to talk to the pupils about what had happened as part of their citizenship education. Speaking to the schoolchildren and hearing their reaction made it clear to us that our experience must not be wasted – we realised that our

Jimmy's story had such an impact and that it should be
shared. This meeting, at a school in Bermondsey, really
represents the beginning of what was to become the
Jimmy Mizen Foundation.

The ethos of the Foundation is that we all, each
one of us, have to work together and play our part for
a more civil, safe society. The aim of the Foundation is
to foster participation of young people as responsible
citizens in their communities, building awareness
about the consequences when there's a breakdown of
respect and an abdication of responsibility and to create
relationships in our community so there is a sense of
collective responsibility for each other and the area in
which we live.

We knew that if we were to create a community that
is safe for all our children, then they needed to be part
of the conversation on how we all achieve it. Speaking
to children about our experience and hearing theirs
is incredibly valuable. We have worked with groups
of schoolchildren of all different ages and developed
a presentation that gives details of what happened to
Jimmy and why it's so important that there is a peaceful
and considered response to crimes of the sort that he
suffered.

It became quite clear to us that if young people feel
that they have a stake in their local community they
will feel some responsibility for it and how it functions.
Given the right guidance and opportunity, young people
who may have been vulnerable to falling into crime can
be diverted from it.

We had seen first-hand how the Scouts can provide
engagement and guidance for young people as Jimmy
had been an active member and so we worked with
them to improve our local area. We fundraised for
minibuses to enable young people to participate in the

Scouts' activities. We now have four "Jimmybuses"
that are used by the youth and other local community
organisations. To tackle the underlying issues of youth
unemployment we've established an apprenticeship
scheme in Jimmy's memory for people from South East
London aged between 18 and 24 and are hoping to
extend it, and develop a work experience programme
with businesses that want to give something back to the
community.

My family has opened a coffee shop in Jimmy's
memory, and a headquarters for the Foundation next
door to it, near our home in Lewisham. The Café
of Good Hope, run by Jimmy's brothers, isn't only a
tribute to our son and a fundraiser for the work of the
Foundation, it is also a safe haven for anyone who feels
under threat or intimidated on the streets. From our
discussions in schools, and with other groups of young
people, it was worrying to discover how many felt a real
fear of crime.

The outpouring of sympathy and love that we
received from members of our community after Jimmy's
death gave us hope that people did care about their
neighbours and the security of the place where they
live and they did want to work to make it better. There
seemed to be a collective feeling that if communities
look out for each other, keep an eye on our streets, know
who local residents are and that there is somewhere
safe for them, we can rebuild the ties that make our
communities safer. That's what the broad-based
community organisation, London Citizens, has tapped
into and we've worked with them to develop City Safe
Havens – sanctuaries for people if they feel unsafe on
the street. We have established more than 200 across
London and are working to roll them out in other parts
of the country.

I think that the fact that Jimmy's murderer, Jake
Fahri, although a known thug, was also a young
member of our community demonstrated to people
that all young people, not just our own children, are in
some way our responsibility. After Jake killed Jimmy
many people, including the press, were suddenly very
interested in how he was going to spend the next two
decades of his life, but I can't help thinking that if we'd
shown the same level of interest in how he spent the
first two decades my son might still be alive. That isn't
to absolve him from responsibility for his crime. I have
no problem with the fact that Jake is now serving a life
sentence for what he did. But I am far more concerned
about what comes out of prison than when it happens.
Will it be the same angry, dysfunctional man or a
reformed member of society?

If I believed that longer sentences served in
harsher conditions worked to deter people from
crime or reformed criminals I would be all in favour
of that approach. But unfortunately it's much more
complex than that. I have worked with the Forgiveness
Project on workshops in prisons to give offenders the
opportunity to address the harm they have caused to
bereaved families like mine. The offenders I meet have
often experienced problems at school, constant run-
ins with authority and addictions to drugs and other
substances. These are problems which have their roots
in early childhood and it is at that time in people's lives
that they need to be addressed.

I do not see the benefit of a criminal justice
system which seeks only retribution for crimes and
not to reform criminals. We need to ensure that when
offenders leave prison they have changed and are able
to play a productive part in society. Understanding
that their crimes have consequences not only for their

own lives but for the victims and their families too is, I believe, an important part of that process.

I am convinced that trying to foster more civility and humanity in all aspects of life – from schools, to the streets, to prisons – is the only way to counter the incivility and violence my son and too many others faced. It's time to have a grown-up discussion about what role each of us, from politicians and the police to ordinary members of the community, can play. That means challenging widely held assumptions and asking big questions about the kind of society we want to be. We hope that this is what the Foundation we established in our son's name will help facilitate in some way. And that's what Jimmy's legacy will be. Not one of vengeance or fear, but one of hope and peace.

# 11

## Wounded Healers

E tenebris lux – "From the darkness comes light"
(motto of Families Utd)

*In the months leading up to the trial Jake was held in HMP Belmarsh, quite a high security establishment, and I often found myself thinking about him, wondering what it was like for him in prison. Was it harsh? Frightening? Miserable? Or was he having a high old time in some kind of cushy health spa? These questions wouldn't leave me alone, and one day, I happened to share my thoughts with a friend from church. I knew he worked in the prison service but I didn't know in what capacity. It turned out he was governor of a prison on the Isle of Sheppey. I had no idea! He told us prison conditions in the main are pretty grim. Then he said, "Why don't you come and see for yourselves?"*

*Barry and I were very nervous before that first visit. We didn't know what to expect. We saw the cells where the prisoners spend their days – small, dingy rooms with a toilet in the corner and a small TV. Often they have to eat their meals in there, three or four to a cell. It made me very sad to think that so many people spend many years in these places, behind door after door, locked with key after key. There was a room where new inmates go when they first come into prison, where they keep an eye on you in case you're contemplating suicide. Even this room was horrible – dingy walls, no sheets on the bed. You can imagine: their thoughts are going haywire, they're close to panic, and they're put in there supposedly to calm down, to prepare them for prison life. I think I'd read too many tabloid stories about prisoners living a life of luxury at the taxpayer's expense; this was nothing like that. It was a grim Victorian dungeon. The inmates asked us why we'd come in. I think they thought we were officials of some sort checking up on them.*

*I felt no pleasure at the idea that Jake was in such a place. He was a "Category A prisoner" – maximum security – and was being held in a kind of prison within a prison at Belmarsh, probably for his own safety. I wondered about his state of mind: was he blaming Jimmy for what had happened? Was he being aggressive to other prisoners? Was he being victimized? I have to say I wasn't actually worrying about him; I thought, if he's victimized, it's probably his own fault.*

*Then, after the trial, we got a letter from the chaplain of a Young Offender Institution, asking us if we would go in and share our story with the youngsters. I was even more nervous this time: how could we stand up in front of prisoners and talk? What did we have to say? What would it achieve? My knees were knocking together as we stood up and began to speak. There were a hundred or so young people sitting in a semi-circle in the prison chapel, mostly sitting back, arms folded, in very defensive postures. We said, "We're not here to lecture you; we're here to tell you our son's story." Barry shared what happened to Jimmy with them. We showed the DVD* A Sparkle of Hope, *a short film about Jimmy's death and our faith made by the Nationwide Christian trust, and a little montage called* Jimmy Through His Life.

*But they listened and asked very articulate questions. There were several groups of Traveller families, all related to each other, and quite a few of them said, "I haven't done anything – I shouldn't be here!" I particularly liked the Irish Traveller kids – very cheeky, but very straightforward. One boy said, "I'm black and if I was to die, no one would care about me." I said, without thinking, "Maybe not, and I fully understand what you're saying, but I care." Another lad, a young black man aged about nineteen, asked to speak to me privately. He was crying and said he wanted to say sorry to the family hurt by his actions. I felt a tremendous empathy for his pain. I said, "If you need to write a letter saying sorry, write it to me. Look into your own heart." When someone's in this situation, they need to forgive themselves, as well as asking for forgiveness. We were asked afterwards by the chaplain, "Did you see a hundred people like the boy who killed your son?" We didn't. We saw a hundred young people that could have been our sons, under different circumstances.*

*After that visit, Barry and I heaved a deep sigh and said to each other, "This definitely feels like the right place for us to be." I couldn't believe we were saying this. The chaplain said that in twenty years working in prisons, he'd never seen anything like it. It amazes me, because I can't see how anyone would say this about me – I'm really so ordinary! It's almost like it's not us they're talking about.*

. . . . . . . . . . . . .

*We'd been invited to go and speak to the children at a Catholic school a few miles from our home before the trial, around Christmas 2008. The school chaplain is a friend of ours. All 400 children and staff were assembled in a huge school hall. I could hear the sound of my shoes clacking on the floor as we walked up to speak, and my knees were trembling. Why are we doing this? What are we going to say? At that point, for legal reasons, we couldn't tell the whole story of what had happened, but we shared as much as we could, and showed some pictures of Jimmy – as a baby in my arms, and older, in his school uniform. We talked about our faith in some depth, how it had held us together as individuals, as a couple, as a family. "Whenever I can't cope," I said, "I pray the Our Father and I pray to the saints." I said that change in our society will come from each and every one of us choosing to stand for peace, not violence. You could have heard a pin drop. There were some deep concerns in that school about gang violence. There were several groups of kids within the school, which transformed into gangs outside the school gates. I think the school was hoping that if we shared our story and spoke about the consequences of violent actions, it might well help some of their students. Schools do an amazing job under difficult circumstances, and the care they demonstrate for their students is to be applauded.*

*Jimmy was the thirteenth teenager to fall victim to fatal violence in London in 2008, and all these murders were committed by other teenagers. We have to start intervening earlier in young people's lives, to prevent them ever getting involved in violent crime. Pretty soon, I was being invited to speak in primary schools and so we had to think carefully about how to talk about Jimmy's death with very young children. We spoke to an infant year at a primary school in Kent, which was very daunting. What do you say to five- and six-year-olds? We hadn't expected such young children, so we had to adapt at the click of a finger. We obviously had to tone down the story so as not to frighten or upset them.*

*I said that I had a bit of a sad story, because my son lost his life because of someone who wasn't very nice to him. We talked about looking after each other in the playground. Their response was phenomenal – so many deep, searching questions! They're like sponges at that age, listening to every word, absorbing everything. I never have to say very much in primary schools. I just let them ask questions, and then try to speak from my heart and give honest answers. They ask, who hurt Jimmy? Where is the person who hurt him? Do you cry a lot? I say, yes, I do sometimes. I say that I think about Jimmy and how nice he was, and that makes me feel better. I say that prisons aren't very nice places. We often talk about actions and consequences: take a life and you will destroy your own life. We talk about how revenge won't solve the problem. We tell the children how important they are, how special and unique they are. I see these beautiful children with their futures ahead of them, some of them with very difficult home lives, and I feel such a longing to protect them. You can often tell the ones who are struggling, because they won't give eye contact.*

*We try to keep the assembly presentation very short in primary schools, just ten minutes, and then we go and talk to the Year Six pupils for longer. We always discuss with the staff beforehand what we're going to say, although it's never the same, because we're responding to their questions, and we like to keep it fresh and spontaneous. I talk about weapons, how it's not just a knife, but it could be anything sharp or heavy that can hurt someone. I say, if you're being bullied, tell someone you can trust, and don't let the bullies win. If you're a bully, hang your head in shame. Children in Years Five and Six will often tell us that they've lost a relative or a friend and they don't know how to deal with it. "My nan died and I am crying and hurting," said one little boy to me once. It's so hard to know what to say. I gave him a hug and asked him to tell me about his nan and then encouraged him to remember all the good times they had, and to try to remember her with a smile, as we remember our Jimmy with a smile. You can see how some of these kids look at you in such pain; the things we're discussing with them are touching deep nerves. We have some wonderful letters from pupils after these visits: "We're so sorry for your loss, you've inspired us, when are you coming again?"*

*Some schools are really challenging, of course. On one visit, we talked to the toughest boys in the school. We asked them, "If you shove people and hurt them and put fear into them, do you think about how they feel that night, or the next day?" It really seemed as though they had never thought about that. They were bright kids, clear of eye, natural leaders, but leading in the wrong direction. We went to a tough secondary school in Bristol, where the teachers asked us to speak to the most troublesome group of kids. We went in and showed Jimmy's pictures and shared our story. We said we weren't there as teachers, just a mum and dad. They all had their feet up on the desks and were really rowdy, not listening, but as we told Jimmy's story and shared our thoughts they became very attentive and showed great empathy towards us. We had spoken of things that had a resonance with many of them and we like to think it has helped in some way.*

*Early intervention is so important because of the tough lives that both parents and children have. Some of these parents are very young. I think back to when I had Joanne, forty years ago; they kept you in hospital for ten days and you were shown how to be a parent, how to bathe and feed your baby. Nowadays you're out after a few hours.*

*Life is quite simple really. What does any of us truly need and want? We just need to know: do I matter? Am I loved? Am I of value? We ask the children this and follow it up with, "Yes, you do matter; yes, you are loved; yes, you are of value – and don't let anyone else tell you otherwise." It always pains us, when we share this, to see some children with tears in their eyes. It's probably hard for most of us to accept that there are children being born in Britain who are not wanted from birth, let alone loved. Why are we so surprised and shocked when they go on to do some of the horrible things they do? It needs to change, and it starts with every one of us; we all have a responsibility for all the children in our society.*

. . . . . . . . . . . . .

*Our next prison invitation was from a prison volunteer who works with the Sycamore Tree Project. This is a really amazing six-week course, in which prisoners are invited to explore their own emotions, accept responsibility for what they have done, and come up with different creative ways of saying sorry. Around the third or fourth week of the project, a victim of crime, or in our case the family of a victim of crime, comes in to share their story, and then returns in the sixth week. At this second meeting, the prisoners have the opportunity to present a letter, a poem or a piece of art or sculpture to the victim's family, who stand there as a kind of surrogate victim's family for all the offenders. We were at Downview, a women's prison, and it was* one of the most emotional visits we've ever made. The prisoners' families are allowed to attend, along with other visitors, so there were quite a lot of people in the room. One young woman was going to lose her children because of what she'd done, and she stood in front of us and said sorry. She was in her mid-twenties, and she had tortured a female friend of hers, done really horrific things to her. She'd had a meeting with Social Services and had to say goodbye to her children that day, because they were being taken into care. She was shaking with emotion. I've never been so deeply touched. She was really a very ordinary-looking person, the kind of young mum you might meet at the school gates. I remember giving her a hug, and later her mother came and thanked me. She was very ordinary-looking as well. There was nothing about either of them that would have given any clue about what had happened. Horrific events and terrible consequences would seem to be never far away.

Part of the course is about helping the participants to accept what they've done, as a first step before saying sorry. A lot of people in prisons are paralysed with self-justification, blaming their victim, blaming other people in their lives for their actions. There was another young girl, in her early twenties, who clearly had some kind of mental illness. She was very nervous, holding her helper's arm all the time, leaning her head on her shoulder, almost unable to speak. She'd decorated a bar of soap with beads, all around the edges and in the middle, and the beads spelled the word, "Sorry." She presented this to us. I did manage to speak with her afterwards, and she shared some of her story. It was distressing, and I wondered what good it was doing her, being locked up.

In the middle of all these women who were coming up to me, presenting us with their pain and guilt, I felt I wanted to stay there and help look after them, protect them. Some of them have had very tough lives. I would have liked to go in every day to be with them.

The next visit was nine months or so after the trial. Barry couldn't come this time, so Danny came with me. He said, "Mum, I'll come in with you, no problem, but I'm not going to speak." When we got there he couldn't stop talking! I was astonished; I really hadn't expected this. He talked about how he's had to live with his brother's death, about how most perpetrators are bullies who've been bullied themselves, about the need to turn their lives around. He's a natural speaker and leader and it felt absolutely right for him *to be there. He saw all those women as ordinary people, not wicked offenders, and he was really keen to come to the final session. The women were really keen too – a 6-foot-4 strapping young handsome fellow – they'd taken quite a shine to Danny!*

*Then came the Seeds of Forgiveness course, also held at Downview Prison, and this time Tommy came. He brought his guitar with him and sang his song "Sparkle"; it had an amazing impact on all the women. We shared Jimmy's story and mingled with them, drank tea with them, and became their friends for an hour or so. A lot of them never have any visitors, although I did get the impression that they are quite close friends with each other. We didn't witness any bickering. The women showed tremendous respect and empathy; I felt they almost wanted to look after me! Seeds of Forgiveness is a creative writing course on the theme of forgiveness, and at the end, they produced a book of poems and reflections written by the prisoners. We were invited back for the launch of this book, and some of the poems were extremely moving. Several referred directly to our visit:*

"In Memory" (extract)
(For the Mizen family, Seeds of Forgiveness project,
June 2009)

Jimmy Mizen –you were taken away
From family and friends
At such a young age…

Your family are loving, caring,
Compassionate, courageous people.
The strength it must have taken
To come into our prison
And talk so openly…

Nothing can be done
To have you back
But still we must go on.

Hearing Barry and Margaret's story
Made me re-think my life…
When I spoke to them,
There was so much I wanted to say.
Their talk inspired me to write this poem,
I hope it reaches out to others,
In memory of –Jimmy Mizen.

CM

"30 Years"

For 30 years I have carried you around on my back
For 30 years your voice has been in my head
For 30 years I've heard "you're useless", "you're pathetic"
For 30 years I have not spoken or seen you
For 30 years I have hated you so much

After 30 years the Mizens have changed all that
After 30 years I can see your pain and anguish
After 30 years I can now forgive you
After 30 years I ask you to forgive me
After 30 years I can leave you in my past
Now, after 30 years, I am free –at last.

MM

*One lady, a Filipina prisoner in her thirties, was very gifted at origami. She'd made a huge bunch of beautiful yellow origami roses, and taught the other prisoners to make them as well. She wanted us to sell them to raise money for the Jimmy Mizen Foundation.*

· · · · · · · · · · · ·

*Not long after this, we were contacted by Marina Cantacuzino, the founder and director of The Forgiveness Project. She'd created an exhibition, The F-Word:*

*Images of Forgiveness, at the Oxo Gallery in 1994, which drew a lot of publicity. The Forgiveness Project works to explore forgiveness, reconciliation and conflict resolution by collecting and sharing stories from real lives, and delivering outreach programmes in schools, prisons, faith communities, and other forums. Their vision is "to create a better future by healing the wounds of the past". Marina wanted to write up our story for their website, so she came and interviewed us, and after that, she invited us to go with her into prisons as part of their course. As usual, we couldn't fathom why she or anyone else would be interested in us. But we went along and shared our story and talked about what we felt forgiveness was. We always get dozens of questions from the prisoners on these visits, always very respectful. One young man asked me how he could forgive himself. I said, "My only answer is that you have to look into your own heart. It will come from there."*

*With The Forgiveness Project, the visit from a victim's family is the first presentation, trying to engage the prisoners with the importance of forgiveness, and inviting them to sign up for a three-day workshop. Seeing our story on their website, and in the materials they give out, alongside amazing stories of forgiveness from South Africa, Northern Ireland, Israel-Palestine, and so on, made us feel honoured to be included. We actually met Desmond Tutu at one of the Forgiveness Project lectures in London, in 2010. He was a lovely man, really so easy-going, no-nonsense, and very funny. You'd never have thought he was one of the greatest heroes of our times.*

. . . . . . . . . . . . .

*Two weeks after Jimmy was killed, another innocent teenage lad was murdered not far from us in south London: Robert Knox, who'd been in several of the Harry Potter films. He'd played rugby for Sidcup and we knew his uncle, so it felt right to do something to express our empathy for the family. We left some flowers and a card at the spot where Rob was killed, and after a little while, his mum Sally rang us and we arranged to meet her and her husband Colin for a meal. Then, some months later, we received an invitation from Gordon Brown to come to 10 Downing Street and meet a group of other families who'd all lost children to violent crime. It was a big moment, in a way, but the reason for the invitation took away any sense of excitement at being invited to the Prime Minister's house. Colin and Sally were there, and Grace* and Tim Idowu, whose son David was also killed in 2008, Kiyan Prince's mum Tracy, and Damilola Taylor's dad Richard. That was the beginning of Families Utd.

Just as when Samantha was born with Down's syndrome, we felt such a need to connect with other families going through the same challenges. All the other families we met at Downing Street felt the same, and so the friendships formed very naturally and we decided to start a support group for families bereaved through violence. Someone from the Damilola Taylor Trust came up with the name Families Utd, and it's grown from that point. The group is there particularly for newly bereaved families, of whom sadly there are so many. They're often bewildered and don't know where to turn. They've read about us in the papers and get in touch because they can't deal with what's happened to them. We share advice and knowledge, but most importantly friendship and comfort. We ask if they'd like to put their child's story on the Families Utd website, and we put them in touch with other bereaved families. This solidarity brings tremendous hope and healing for many.

It's not just families of people killed on our own streets that we meet. The family of a renowned photojournalist killed in Libya, Tim Hetherington, got in touch. His mother had seen a poster for a talk we were giving at a church in London. She and her husband lived in Manchester, and we got an email though the Families Utd website asking if there was anyone they could talk to. The pain of losing their son was overwhelming. We arranged to meet them in Hyde Park, and talked together for a long time and shared stories about our children. They told us later that for them to hear that we were experiencing the same emotions and feelings was a great help. "Do you think about Jimmy?" they asked. "Every thought, every feeling, every action, and every word we now speak is different since our Jimmy's death," we said. This resonated greatly with them and we hope has helped them in some way to find a small measure of healing from such a great loss. These experiences redefine who you are. We give a lot to Families Utd, but I'm sure we receive more in return. Helping others who are going through the same anguish helps us in a way that goes beyond words.

. . . . . . . . . . . . .

Justin Butcher:

I'm sitting in the common room of a prison in Oxfordshire with Margaret and Barry and two dozen young men in prison fatigues. They are a mixture of British Asian, British Caribbean, and white, mostly in their early twenties. Some are bright and attentive, some withdrawn, some look positively disturbed. Many are heavily tattooed on their arms and faces, but all have one thing in common: they are serving long sentences, many for murder. We're here to talk about forgiveness.

Colette, a smartly dressed young woman who works for HMP Huntercombe as an educational coordinator, gets up to welcome Marina Cantacuzino, who at first sight seems an unlikely spokeswoman for such an initiative as remarkable as The Forgiveness Project: tall, slim, fiftyish, she is not overtly warm, certainly not gushy. If anything, her demeanour is reserved, even austere. She speaks with an understated, focused confidence and I'm impressed by the trust she places in her audience of "lifers"to grasp what she's saying. There's nothing ingratiating or patronizing in her delivery; she expects these men to attend to and engage with what she's saying, and they do.

Forgiveness, she says, is not something you do for other people. You do it for yourself, to set yourself free from victimhood and to end your dependency on the perpetrator of your hurt. As long as you continue to hate, or desire revenge upon, the one who hurt you, you are still in their power. As long as you refuse to accept the truth of what happened to you, then the past will dominate and define your present, and your future.

I'm fascinated by these ideas as they float out in her very unsensational style of presentation, and her audience is following every word. Many of these guys have killed someone, I remind myself – but she's not here to tell them all to repent, to apologize, to beg forgiveness for what they've done. This is about them learning how to forgive – forgiving those who've damaged them in the past, and crucially, forgiving themselves. I look round at these scarred, tattooed faces which, despite their youth, look so careworn, old before their time, some haunted, some almost wise. Marina's proposition – that their first need is to contemplate whom and what they themselves need to forgive – strikes me as an astonishingly radical notion. If it caught on, it could turn our criminal justice system upside down.

Marina shows them a documentary film, *The F-Word*, which draws together many extraordinary testimonies of forgiveness from around the world, in a stylishly shot, moody sequence of stills, interviews, graphics, and music. It ends with an image of a young man sitting in a cell, lit only in silhouette, his head in his hands, as broken phrases materialize and dissolve:

Forgiveness

Forgiveness means giving

Forgiveness means giving up

Forgiveness means giving up all hope

Forgiveness means giving up all hope of a better past

Barry and Margaret get up to speak, introduced by Marina. They summarize briefly the events of Jimmy's death, and speak movingly of their conviction that the answer to violent tragedy is not retribution, but forgiveness and hope. They allude to their faith in a low-key manner: "This is part of who we are, and we understand forgiveness as part of our faith, but we don't say that you have to have a faith in order to forgive or be forgiven." The prisoners are respectful and attentive, and ask some searching questions. "Have you ever met the person who killed your son?" asks one. "No," replies Margaret, "but I believe everyone deserves to be forgiven, even the killer of my son. I look at you all, and you could be my own children."

It's hard to convey the awe and astonishment that this statement provokes, the intensity of brimming emotions –pain, hope, regret, shame, gratitude – with which the atmosphere in the room is now charged. "I don't believe anyone should make excuses for me," says one deep-voiced, burly young man. "I believe I should take responsibility for what I done." As Marina often observes, being under judgment themselves, many prisoners harbour extremely judgmental attitudes towards each other and themselves.

There's a discussion about poverty or deprivation as one of the causes of crime. I mention the recent case of the gay civil servant, Ian Baynham, who was punched and kicked to death by three teenagers, two girls and a boy, in Trafalgar Square in September 2009. Not everyone convicted of murder necessarily has a deprived background; in this case, one of the teenage girls had been to a number of exclusive private schools. "Yeah, but you're assuming she was cared for by her parents," retorts one of the prisoners. "She might have been abandoned, neglected, even though they had lots of money. You can't make assumptions!" I acknowledge his point.

After the formal presentation is over, every single prisoner goes up to shake hands with Margaret and Barry, thanking them for their visit. There's something in the gift of their openness as a couple, the absence of anger, that somehow enables these men to come forward to them. It's amazingly permissive, a sign of grace. One young man, British Asian, speaks privately to Margaret for a long time, clinging to her, seeming overwrought with emotion, sweating and trembling. Margaret listens, holding his hand, as he pours out his heart.

"I found it very moving," says Margaret later, "and distressing in a way. I almost thought he needed to go on suicide watch. He was saying he'd done the course before, but he didn't know how to forgive himself. And I hope and pray that's something he would come to. I didn't have any feelings of hate towards him at all. I felt I wanted to take him in my arms, to be honest with you, because there was no look in his eyes of wanting to do it again. I sensed a real feeling that he was sorry, but didn't know how to forgive himself. His whole body was in a hot sweat; you could almost feel his heart pounding. He was just trying to say, 'I can't forgive myself', but he couldn't get the words out. So, to me, there's someone who is ready for the change.

He's been in prison for nine years, and you felt that if he was to come out, he probably wouldn't do it again.

"We condemn, but God doesn't condemn."

. . . . . . . . . . . . .

*In November 2010, on "Prison Sunday", we visited HMP Swinfen Hall, in Staffordshire. It's one of the three Young Offender Institutions in the UK where all the prisoners are serving life sentences, many for murder. They take youngsters up to the age of twenty-five. These young lads didn't know what to expect; they were very defensive at the start, all sitting back in their chairs with their arms folded. They listened very, very thoughtfully while we were talking, then afterwards, one young man put up his hand and said, "I'm a Jake sort of person. I did to someone what Jake did to Jimmy. I'm so, so sorry. I keep trying to write a letter to the family and say how sorry I am. I've written that letter so many times but I can't bring myself to send it."*

*So I said, "Why don't you write it and send it to us?" And he did. We were completely bowled over. This is an extract from his letter:*

> Saturday 20 November 2010
> HMP Swinfen Hall
> Lichfield
> Staffordshire
> WS14 9QS
>
> Dear Mr and Mrs Mizen,
>
> I'm writing this letter to thank you for the touch you have placed on my life. I am currently in prison for murder and doing life with a minimum of 16 years… I am now 20 years old, but at the age of 17 I made the worst mistake a boy could make.
>
> [He describes his crime.] This was a shameful day. The worst day of my life…
>
> You advised me to at least try and send a letter to the parents of [the boy I killed]… I've actually wrote

hundreds of sorry letters since before I was even convicted. But once finished, each letter eventually gets screwed up and put in the bin. They have just never felt like enough... the sad, unbearable truth always hits home, that no sorry will ever do, no matter how strongly felt. I can't ever make up for what I'm responsible for. No matter how much I twist and turn on my bed at night and beg God to rewind time or swap me for [the boy I killed]. No matter what I ever do in life, my undeserving life, nothing will ever, can ever truly make up for a life lost. Nothing...

I've been in prison for coming up to four years and I don't think I've ever met one of the evil people I used to read about in newspapers. Maybe I'm still young to prison, I don't know, but the evil people the media seem to talk about after every conviction, don't seem to really exist. Or surely not in the amounts projected anyway. But these are just my thoughts. I ain't no psychologist and I definitely ain't no philosopher. I'm just Xxxxx from Wapping, East London. Just over the bridge from you. I just got tangled up in a web of fictional thought as a teenager and after a shameful catalogue of crimes in my deluded world of war, drink and drugs, I'm now just a person in a cell. To many, an undeserving-of-life piece of scum. Whether that's a true observation or not is irrelevant to me, because I understand its perspective.

In 2009 January, I was on *Panorama* ("Jailed for a Knife") talking about knife crime. I was being interviewed by a good man called Raphael Rowe and he asked me a question I will never forget. He said, "The parents of your victim and others say you should have received the death penalty, what do you say to that?" This question, although I'd heard its content before, left me speechless. I can't remember my answer, but it just reminded me of how much I was really hated. Growing up as a kid I never thought how one day soon I'd be hated by good ordinary people on such a level...

Although I have thought about it a lot, I would never kill myself and have never tried... maybe my life is the flame of pain in many's grief and to out it would be cooling for many. But the arguments against this logic mostly seem to outweigh the arguments for it. My mum and dad, although heartbroken, have always been there for me and always will. I could never be the cause of any more pain to them. My little sister still prays for me, and my older brother still wells up when talking of old times.

... people like you are true examples of human beings. All should strive to be like you. I chose good a long time back before I was even convicted, but I've had hiccups mostly due to my hostile environment, but this is no excuse, I allowed myself to be sucked in on occasions... Some people may look at you and think your faith, tolerance and ability to forgive are just components born from a great pain that help you deal with it. And this may be true. But I saw something stronger than reaction working within you both today. You both lit up my world and I just want to say thanks.

You complement each other's presence with a dignity and grace I can only wish to the stars to one day have with someone. The work you are doing and have done is I believe beyond comprehension. I don't think anyone can truly understand and maybe not even yourselves, the true content and scale of the effect you and your work radiate. And I believe this letter should be a surprise to you for I didn't say much today, and if this is a surprise then it's evidence of what I just said.

My mind has been at battle with my heart for a long time over God's existence. And maybe the battles between my mind & heart will wage many times more in my future, I don't know. But today you showed me who will win that war.

Today God showed me you.
And today you showed me God.
Thank you.

Xxxxx Xxxxx Xxxxx

•  •  •  •  •  •  •  •  •  •  •  •

*This work has just evolved organically; none of it's been planned. We've never asked to go into a school or prison; we've always been invited. We would love to do more prison visits, but it's very costly for us, as most prisons have no budget for this kind of thing. Throughout that first year after Jimmy's death, we had a group of friends fundraising in Jimmy's memory, initially for the minibus for the local Scouts group, which became known as the "Jimmybus". Over that time, we were becoming aware of a strong sense of our calling, or vocation: to engage with children before they get involved in violence and crime, and to reach out to those whose lives have been scarred by crimes, both victims and perpetrators. The strength of what we do is our ordinariness. I have nothing to win or lose in these situations. I'm doing this work because I know the pain of losing a child. I don't want to hear of any more children dying.*

*If I'm really honest, I'd just like to have Jimmy back.*

# 12

# The Papal Vigil

Justin Butcher:

In the months leading up to the four-day state visit of Pope Benedict XVI in September 2010, I was approached by the Catholic Agency for Overseas Development (CAFOD). They asked me to help them programme and produce a huge event: a multi-media celebration of the Catholic faith in the UK and overseas for a live audience of 80,000 people, plus news media, at the Papal Vigil in Hyde Park on 18 September 2010. This presentation, combining film sequences, live music and worship, drama, and live testimonies from Catholic believers of all walks of life, would occupy the final hour before the arrival of Pope Benedict in Hyde Park. He would then lead a candlelit vigil of prayer, reflection, and worship, focusing on the life and teachings of the great English nineteenth-century thinker, scholar, poet, and religious reformer Cardinal John Henry Newman, who was to be beatified the next day, 19 September, in Birmingham. Beatification is an honour conferred on great figures of faith by the Catholic Church, which celebrates their entry into heaven and affirms the belief that they now intercede for, or speak to God on behalf of, believers here on earth who pray in their name. Beatification is the third step on the path to canonization, being recognized as a saint, and confers the title "Blessed" on the individual.

Working closely with CAFOD and the Catholic Bishops'Conference of England and Wales, we began to develop a script for the event, exploring and interrogating the phrase chosen as the theme and title of the Papal visit, Newman's motto, "Heart speaks unto heart." There was a clear sense that, if the event was to celebrate the breadth and depth of the Catholic community in the UK and beyond, it must represent and include the widest possible scope of Catholic laity, people living out their faith at the coal-face, often in extreme or challenging circumstances, in the mess and detail of everyday life. So, we had testimonies from a sixteen-year-old campaigner for human rights in Burma, Declan Stokle; a Malawian asylum seeker, Ethel Singo, recently released, with her family, from a detention centre in Lancashire; a prison chaplain, Julia Houlston-Clark, working in restorative justice in Cardiff, and a young actor, Kerry Norridge, previously a heroin addict for ten years, whose life had been turned around by the Cardinal Hume project in Westminster. The prayers were led by five schoolchildren from around the UK. The Nigerian actor Israel Oyelamude performed a spectacular solo rendition of the Beatitudes from Matthew's Gospel. The compères were TV *Countdown* celebrity Carol Vorderman and the writer Frank Cottrell Boyce. But the highlight of the event was undoubtedly the testimony of Margaret and Barry Mizen.

My colleagues at CAFOD had told me about their story and their work, but as I travelled down to Lee to meet them for the first time in June 2010, I was apprehensive. We were putting together a presentation – producing a show, in essence – that had to do justice to the life of the Catholic community across the UK. It had to run strictly to time, to synchronize with the Pope's arrival in Hyde Park (a high-security operation), and to satisfy the requirements (and allay the concerns) of numerous partners and organizers – the Foreign & Commonwealth Office, the Vatican, the Metropolitan Police and the Royal Parks, as well as CAFOD and the Bishops' Conference. And all this in the full glare of the media spotlight: there would be over 200 international news organizations covering the event. There was an increasingly hostile atmosphere in the UK media about the cost of this state visit to the British taxpayer (estimated at anything from £10 million upwards), and news revelations breaking on an almost daily basis about child abuse cover-ups amongst Catholic clergy in Ireland, the UK, and the US.

Would the Mizens be able to cope with this level of public exposure, on such a huge stage? Would their testimony "work" in the context of the "show"? Would it connect, through TV monitors, with such a gigantic audience? What if it didn't? Would they be willing to work with me, effectively, as their "director"?

My concerns evaporated instantly on meeting them. They were warm and relaxed, and welcomed me into their family kitchen. We drank tea around their kitchen table and chatted about the Hyde Park event and what would be involved. They showed me the huge collage of photographs of Jimmy on the wall, and shared some of his story with me. I mentioned my own background of family tragedy: aged nineteen, in 1988, I had lost my father and brother, both drowned while the three of us were fishing together off the north coast of Cornwall. I alluded to my own lifelong journey of faith, in the Anglican tradition. I found them wonderfully easy-going, accommodating, and un-precious. "We're really happy to do whatever you need for the event," they said. "We'll do five minutes, three minutes, whatever." One snag was that they weren't used to working with a script – "We always prefer to speak off the cuff, to keep it spontaneous, natural" – which is fine in a school assembly or a prison chapel, but not for an event on this scale. When speaking to an audience of 80,000 through a vast PA, monitored on giant screens, succinct impact is everything. Every word has to count. If you clam up, or flounder, or start repeating yourself, it could be a disaster.

We agreed that we'd do a dry run, with some of the other participants, in a large rehearsal room, at which Margaret and Barry could improvise their testimony without the pressure of an audience or time constraints. I'd have someone standing by transcribing everything they said, and from this together we would develop a script as back-up in case inspiration faltered on the day.

Margaret and Barry of course got along instantly with all the other participants, and our star compères Carol and Frank were great collaborators, easy-going, friendly, and ultra-professional. They both contributed very creatively to the script, structure, and staging of the event and, come the day, they held the vast, potentially unwieldy carnival together with great chutzpah and stamina, finessing the transitions from rowdy youth pageants processing across the stage, to Roma gypsy dance troupes, to huge orchestras and choirs, through to the climactic arrival of the Pope himself.

• • • • • • • • • • • •

Fast forward to the final hour before the Pope's arrival. All going well so far. A glorious, sunny late summer's day in Hyde Park. No terrorist attacks and no noticeable disturbance from the (relatively small) groups of protestors on Park Lane. The crowd was every bit as huge as predicted. The backstage village, run by a tribe of event management techies, was like an impregnable medieval fortress built out from the back of the enormous stage. Massive TV monitors framed the crowd at the front and down either side, around a field covered with a square mile of humanity. The stage looked rather like a set from an old Hollywood movie, in technicolour – red and gold colonnades, a massive throne, an enormous cross upstage centre, and the biggest altar I've ever seen. Carol and Frank were on great form, formally welcoming the crowd that had been gathering all afternoon, with roars of approval from different sections when the names of their cities or towns were called out. Declan, Ethel, and Kerry had all done well, each testimony gaining warm recognition from the audience. Composer Edwin Fawcett was doing a great job with the music; the band and choir were superb. Israel Oyelamude had taken the Beatitudes passage by the scruff of its neck and beaten the dust out of it till it caught fire, striding about the stage and crying out the story in a rich, declamatory, sing-song delivery that seemed to plumb every note of the scale. Now it was Margaret and Barry's turn. "Break a leg," I whispered to them in the wings. "You'll be fine."

As the couple walked to centre stage, flanked by Tommy and George, the vast audience hushed to a pin-drop silence. Barry spoke first:

"My name is Barry Mizen and I'm here today with my wife Margaret and two of our sons, Tommy and George. We come from the parish of Our Lady of Lourdes in Lee, south-east London" – a cheer went up from one section of the crowd, close to the front – "and we wish to talk about our son, Jimmy Mizen, who was murdered in May 2008."

He described briefly the events surrounding Jimmy's death, then went on:

"We've become a nation that is far too ready to commit anger and confrontation, and it doesn't have to be like this. And we, in Jimmy's memory, want to bring something good out of what happened to our dear son. Myself and my wife, we now visit schools and prisons and we talk of Jimmy, but more importantly, we send a message of peace. And if we want peace in our communities, we can't wait for the government or the police or indeed our marvellous church leaders to do this for us. This is something each and every one of us has to do."

Applause broke out at this last comment, and swept across the crowd, as Barry continued:

"So I would urge everyone here, when we return to our parishes, to do whatever we can to work for peace for the common good. The person who killed my son released anger. We must release peace."

Prolonged applause, and great cheers of support, rose from the crowd, as Barry gave place at the lectern to his wife. Putting on her glasses to read her testimony, Margaret turned briefly to smile at her husband – "OK?" – and, at his nod, she began:

"Jimmy died the day after his sixteenth birthday. He went off that morning to buy his first ever lottery ticket, and we were laughing about it just before he went out."

The big screens showed an image of Margaret and Jimmy at a party, both smiling broadly, his arm around his mother's shoulder, her head tucked beneath his chin.

"Five minutes later I got a phone call: 'Get round the corner quick. Jimmy's been attacked.' I ran round the corner and saw all the commotion, and I was screaming, 'Where's Jimmy? Where's Jimmy?' It was very hard to grasp what was going on. I'm the mother of nine children; they were telling me that one of my beautiful children had been murdered."

To her right, Barry stood, looking down, hands clasped in front of his suit jacket, and to his right, George stood in identical pose, equally smart in school blazer and tie, a pained, absent expression on his face.

"When we eventually got home, there must have been at least 200 people gathered in our house. I had to go up to the bedroom, just to try and make sense of what was going on. The only thing I could think of was that my son was now in heaven with God."

A picture of Jimmy on a campsite came up on the screens, grinning incorrigibly at the camera, squinting in the sunlight, between two pitched tents.

"I felt the real presence of the Lord there, and prayed and prayed the Hail Mary and the Our Father, and I knew that Jimmy was safe. The pain was unbearable, but we got through those awful times, particularly the next couple of days. But to this day, I still know my son is safe in heaven."

As if receding into memory, the picture cross-faded slowly with the live monitored image of Margaret at the lectern.

"The next day, at church, we received an immense outpouring of love from so many people coming up to us, crying on our shoulders. The comfort they brought us was amazing. God is good and works in the most wonderful ways. Over the following weeks, the response from our parish was equally amazing: endless food was brought round, washing and housework done, our son George here, he was picked up from school – this was all part of God's work.

"After we left church, there were a lot of press waiting for us, asking us questions. Neither of us knew what was going on, and we'd never really had anything to do with the press, so it was a bit of a shock. But one of the things we said was we didn't feel angry. No one could understand our reaction, but we had learned very quickly that anger breeds anger. It was anger that killed our son and we wouldn't allow it to destroy our family. So we were determined not to be angry about what happened to Jimmy. It is so very easy to start shouting and pointing the finger of blame, but this was not what we wanted to do. But we were very sad, and at times the pain was unbearable."

Startlingly, the screens showed a picture of Jimmy at his First Communion, aged perhaps eight or nine, ears sticking out beneath pudding-basin haircut, dark eyes unmistakable, in smart trousers, shirt and tie, standing in front of an altar bedecked with candles, flowers, and embroidered cloths, a scarlet sash running from his left shoulder down to his right hip. Jimmy's gaze has strayed off to one side, as he idly bends and stretches his right forefinger against his left thumb, while to his left a little girl in white satin dress, with tiara Alice-band and white feathers in her hair, smiles dutifully, if awkwardly, into the camera.

"But this is my message to you parents: please, take your children in your arms and tell them how much you love them, how precious they are, how proud you are of them… And to all you young people out there, I would say: please be proud of your faith, as our Jimmy was. On Sundays he'd come to church, sometimes a few minutes late, but he'd go up for communion and give us such a big smile. Or when Barry and I were doing our daily readings in the mornings, he'd sit with us at the table, not at all embarrassed. So please, be proud of your faith, and remember that God is always with you.

"And finally, as part of Jimmy's legacy, I would ask everyone here to please remember him and all victims of violent crime, with a hope for the future, not for anger, but for peace, where no more kind, gentle, young people are taken from us.

"You know, it was a privilege and a pleasure to have been the parents of Jimmy Mizen, and we feel so honoured. But I'd also like to say one last thing: it's a big thank you to each and every one of you, for all the love that you gave us through our terrible time. God bless you all."

These words, transcribed to the page, cannot convey the scale of the collective emotion invoked in that moment. As Margaret concluded her testimony, 80,000 people rose to their feet as one and applauded. Throughout the afternoon, there had been plenty of high-spirited applause for the many choirs, dance groups, orchestras, and processions occupying the stage, but this was different. There was no whooping or cheering, but a quality of solemnity, born of deep empathy and admiration, and the applause went on and on, for several minutes. Eventually, Edwin Fawcett began to play the opening chords to the stirring anthem by Rolf Løvland and Brendan Graham, "You Raise Me Up", but still the applause went on. The well-known school portrait shot of Jimmy in blazer and tie filled the screens, as a gospel singer stood forward and sang:

> When I am down and, oh my soul, so weary,
> When troubles come and my heart burdened be,
> Then I am still and wait here in the silence,
> Until you come and sit awhile with me.
>
> You raise me up, so I can stand on mountains;
> You raise me up, to walk on stormy seas;
> I am strong, when I am on your shoulders;
> You raise me up…to more than I can be.

As the statuesque singer, resplendent in scarlet dress, sang these words to the Irish air "Danny Boy", and the orchestration grew and the gospel choir's voices rose to swell the refrain, Jimmy's portrait remained fixed, the light reflected in his brown eyes like spots of tincture in an icon, his mouth just breaking into a smile, an instant caught in the opening and closing of a camera shutter, for ever young, unchanging, innocent. The song had become a prayer to Jimmy.

> There is no life – no life without its hunger;
> Each restless heart beats so imperfectly.
> But when you come and I am filled with wonder,
> Sometimes I think I glimpse eternity.
> You raise me up…

In his youth, his gentleness, and in the tragic untimely brutality of his death, Jimmy Mizen, raised up in the hearts of the crowd, was himself raising up the gathered Catholic community of Britain in that moment. It almost seemed that we were witnessing the creation of a "folk saint" before our eyes, here in Hyde Park.

And this is how Margaret in particular has come to view Jimmy —as "our saint", interceding in heaven for them and for all families bereaved by the tragic loss of a child. This helps to explain her conviction that Jimmy's death was, in some mysterious way, part of God's plan, and perhaps accounts for her unusual expression:

"It was a privilege and a pleasure to have been the parents of Jimmy Mizen, and we feel so honoured."

But as Barry poignantly observes, as the "cords" connecting him to Jimmy's earthly life are cut, as Jimmy "ascends" to sainthood in heaven, those who remain must live with an almost insupportable tension, straddling the two eras, before and after Jimmy's death. Their life has changed irrevocably, and the cherished scenes from Jimmy's childhood, preserved in anecdotes, photographs, and almost unbearably poignant reels of cine film, are like memories from a lost world.

# 13

# Ambassadors of Peace

*"Every man for himself and God for us all!" laughs Francis, our driver. "That's what we say here — and if you want to use your phone, make sure you close your window!"*

*We're being driven through the plush, green suburbs of up-town Nairobi, myself and Barry, our son Danny, and our friend and co-author Justin Butcher, jammed shoulder to shoulder in a smart white jeep. We have to crane our necks to look out through the windows, which are rather low and small; we've been advised to keep them wound up. We're on a smooth, well-made road, running between bright green grass verges watered with sprinklers, with lots of colourful flowers and shrubs. The soil is bright orange-red, like terracotta bricks, and there are tall date palms and papaya trees on both sides, filled with squawking green parrots and huge black storks with long red bills. These black storks seem to be everywhere in Kenya. We're passing huge, swanky houses, well back from the road on either side, behind high walls and fancy wrought-iron gates, with little guard huts and CCTV cameras. Private security is big business in Kenya, Francis tells us.*

*"Look, this is our State House!" he says. We're driving along the perimeter of a huge, walled estate, with a private road running through parkland towards a large white mansion with red roofs. "Who lives there?" we ask. "It's the Presidential residence!" he exclaims, laughing. He always laughs when he speaks, with crooked gaps in his teeth, giving him a slightly rascally look. He's taken to calling us Mum and Dad, and Danny his brother. "Are you sure he's ours, dear?" says Barry at one point. "He seems a bit different from the others." Francis hoots. Joking apart, we're very conscious of standing out as white people here in Nairobi, particularly with our very tall son Danny.*

*We're leaving the State House behind now and heading steeply downhill, past a tatty-looking university campus, with washing hung out on every balcony. "The University of Nairobi is a corruption-free zone!" reads a large billboard. "Oh well, that's all right then," says Barry. We're off to visit Korogocho, one of the huge slums of Nairobi, where CAFOD works in partnership with the local Catholic churches to support a number of peace and justice projects. We met the local CAFOD staff yesterday and shared our story with them, and then they drove us to a vantage point high up in the city, where we could look down on a panoramic view of the slums. It was like nothing we've ever seen: miles upon miles of little mud huts, with tin roofs, stretching in all directions. It's hard to believe that real people live there – and that we're going to visit some of them.*

*These slums have been the battleground for some of the worst tribal violence in Africa in the last few years. The CAFOD staff have explained the background to us. After the national elections in December 2007, President Kibaki (whose house we've just passed) was returned to office despite widespread rumours that he'd won fewer votes than his rival, Raila Odinga. Kibera, the largest slum in Nairobi (or anywhere in Africa), is in Odinga's constituency, and many Kiberans voted for him. Their sense of outrage at the election result was manipulated by politicians going into the slums handing out money and weapons and encouraging people to riot. Odinga's supporters, who are mostly from the Luo tribe, turned on their neighbours from the Kikuyu tribe, who were supposed to have supported Kibaki. The violence raged for two months, spreading all over Kenya: homes and businesses were looted and burned, women and children raped, thousands killed, hundreds of thousands displaced. Eventually the UN Secretary-General Kofi Annan managed to bring the two sides to the table to negotiate a peace agreement. Odinga was made Prime Minister and head of a power-sharing cabinet, and the violence ended, but in the slums, people had to start trying to rebuild their communities with little or no help from the politicians who'd started it all. Whole villages had been destroyed, houses looted, friendships betrayed; neighbours no longer trusted each other. Young men from one family had killed young men from other families, just across the street. How could anyone look anyone else in the face?*

*In Kibera, two local CAFOD partners, the Kibera Youth Community Programme and the Kenya Youth Foundation (KYF), came together immediately to launch "Operation Hope". They created peace forums and have trained young volunteers in reconciliation skills and set up a crisis centre for trauma counselling. CAFOD has invited us to come and visit some of these projects and share our story with them.*

*To be honest, I'm not sure what we've got to offer them, and I feel pretty nervous, but we'll do our best. It all feels so strange. When we arrived at the airport two days ago, on Sunday morning (11 September), I felt as if we were entering a different world. The airport was very old-fashioned: old wooden panelling everywhere, hundreds of airport staff in uniform hanging around, seemingly not doing very much, and a slightly threatening atmosphere. When we were going through security and buying our visas, the guy on the desk was putting our money into his own pocket, which seemed a bit odd. On the taxi ride from the airport, the roads were packed with people cooking and selling corn on the cob, people sleeping, people urinating, and when we arrived at our hotel, there were armed guards in military uniforms scanning the car for bombs. We hadn't expected that! Once we were inside, the Silver Springs Hotel felt like an oasis – calm, clean, and everything beautifully laid out. The staff were very polite and helpful.*

*Our host and guide is Tom O'Connor, CAFOD's UK Director of Communities and Supporters. He takes us off almost straight away that morning to the university's Catholic Chaplaincy, where we attend a very lively, exuberant Mass, with lots of singing and dancing. Before we went in, we were having a walk around the streets near the church, and a smart, clean-cut young man in sports clothes came up and shook hands with Tom and Barry. Then, quick as a flash, he ripped my necklace from round my neck and tore off down the road. He looked back, as he was running away, with a broad grin on his face, almost defying us to do something. I felt really shaken for a few seconds, then I quickly covered it up: "I'm fine, I'm all right, really, it's nothing. Let it go." I didn't want Tom to think I couldn't cope. My sister Lynny had given me that necklace after Jimmy was killed – a diamond cross on a gold chain. It was very precious to me, but I thought, "Let it go. You can't hang on to possessions." But the incident didn't exactly help us to feel relaxed in this strange, new place. What on earth are we doing here?*

. . . . . . . . . . . . .

"The day after Jimmy Mizen was murdered," writes Tom O'Connor, "I watched his family on the BBC news as they left Sunday Mass and faced the waiting journalists and their cameras. I was captivated and moved by the words of his parents.I could not imagine the pain they carried, and yet they spoke with dignity and faith about a desire that some goodness and peace should come from the terrible loss of their son. There was no hint of wanting revenge. Neither was there any saccharine piety that denied the awful reality of what had happened. Just ordinary people, like you or me, unintentionally offering a profound example of goodness that shone through the darkness of unspeakable human tragedy.

"Two years later I met Margaret and Barry for the first time. CAFOD was helping to prepare the Hyde Park Papal Vigil, which was a major event during the visit of Pope Benedict to the UK. We wanted to hear the stories of how a range of Catholics live their faith in the UK today to inspire reflection among their fellow pilgrims. Margaret and Barry were among those we invited.

"Once again I listened to Jimmy's parents speak about their experience: how the murder of their son was a senseless release of anger and violence, how in response they wanted to release peace, not more anger, and how they found the strength to work for this because of their Catholic faith. And once again I felt humbled and inspired by the goodness and courage of their message.It struck me that the peace for which they were striving was the same peace being sought by people who lived through the post-election riots of 2008 in Kenya – the year of Jimmy's death. They gave a human voice to the peace for which so many people in our world were longing.

"I had already seen the work of CAFOD's partners in Kenya after the violence of 2008. They were ordinary local people driven by the desire to bring peace and reconciliation to their communities and determined not to allow violence to breed hatred and further violence. Parents had lost their children to random tribal killings;families were driven from their burning homes, carrying nothing,with nowhere to run.But this inhumanity would not have the final word, because good people who valued the dignity of every human life would not stop working for peace.

"That is why I invited Margaret and Barry to visit Kenya.They had a story to share that would inspire their brothers and sisters in Nairobi and beyond. There were mothers for them to meet whose sons had been murdered, who were looking to the future with hope. There were young people to meet who had terrorized their neighbourhoods and were now determined to bring back peace and reconciliation."

. . . . . . . . . . . . .

*We swing down past the Catholic Chaplaincy, where we attended the Mass two days ago, and plunge headlong into a huge road crammed with vehicles, all jostling in a massive free-for-all slalom. This is Ngara Road, and it couldn't be more different from the plush, leafy suburbs just a mile back up the hill. There's a pile of enormous boulders down the middle as a central reservation. The road surface is covered with craters and hummocks, and we're all clinging on for dear life as our jeep jolts and bumps and lurches its way through a log-jam of cars, handcarts, and Toyota minibuses packed with passengers. These are called "matatus" – a kind of local taxi – and they scramble and shove backwards and forwards across the lanes (actually there aren't any lanes), trying to get through the traffic. It's every man for himself, Francis reminds us. There are roadside stalls and shops everywhere, with earth walls and corrugated iron roofs, and piles of rubbish, and pedestrians carrying massive sacks through traffic, and here and there you see quite smartly dressed young people striding along, going about their business. Every so often we pass really huge holes in the ground that you could disappear into, car, passengers, and all, if you weren't careful.*

*There seems to be a lot of road-building going on: lots of parked lorries and machinery and piles of construction materials. Back from the roadside, alleyways of stalls covered with dusty awnings and wooden poles, stretching back into the slums. There are shack-shops, shack-cafés and shack-chapels and churches on all sides, with titles painted in large letters on the walls –the Good Hope Shop, the Jesus Upliftance Ministry, the Jehovah Hire Chemist. It's difficult to know whether anything's open, functioning, or derelict. Everything looks derelict. Some of the names are wonderfully grand: the Royal Supermarket (a shack), the Hollywood Butchery (a shack with chickens pecking and clucking out the front), the Glory Cybercafe, the Beverley Hills Hostel. I don't fancy the look of the meat hanging up outside the butchery, entrails and all, with flies all over it.*

*There's business and trade going on everywhere. We're driving past 20 yards of rubbish distributed along the roadside, with flies buzzing all over it and black storks pecking through the plastic bags, then suddenly we see an old woman setting out tomatoes for sale, piling them up like a pyramid on a tea-towel spread on the ground. Then, out of nowhere, there's a huge mountain of smart, shiny furniture piled high: beds hand-made from imported mahogany heaped up higgledy-piggledy on top of bright-patterned upholstered armchairs, for hundreds of yards. Then a long line of funeral-parlour shacks, with carpenters out front building coffins and stacking them up for sale. "Looks like business is booming in the coffin trade," says Barry. "Always!" says Francis, chuckling. I hadn't expected any of this. I think I'd imagined people standing crying by the roadside with begging bowls, the kind of clichéd images you associate with charity appeals.*

*We're heading into Huruma slum. The first thing we see is a new primary school, with a plaque on the wall: "Congratulations to the construction workers and the city councillors whose distinguished effortsbrought this school into being." Next, we're crawling past hundreds of plants for sale, little palm trees and shrubs all tidily bagged up in black plastic and laid out in rows. We've seen lots of these roadside plant nurseries in Nairobi; gardening must be popular here. Now we're passing row upon row of neatly stacked little pots of charcoal briquettes. Suddenly, through a gap in the line of shacks, we get a shocking view of Mathare slum —a huge shanty-town of brown tin roofs stretching down to the Nairobi River and up the other side, with a few tatty breeze-block tenements here and there.*

*Our local guide is Lauretta, a very bright and determined young Kenyan woman from the Luhya tribe, who works for CAFOD in Nairobi. She grew up in the slums herself, she tells us. Her father was a hard-working civil servant, who left his family back in the Nakuru region in the west of Kenya to come and work in Nairobi as a government meteorologist. To save as much of his salary as possible, he rented a small shack during the week in Kibera and went back home at weekends. When she was a teenager, Lauretta came to live with him, to attend school and university in Nairobi. You can't just build your own place in the slums, she explains: even though the settlements look so ramshackle and improvised, in fact every single shack, hut, shed, lean-to, beam, board, fence, and ditch is owned by someone – a landlord or racketeer making money hand over fist at the expense of the poor.*

*In the middle of the next crossroads sits a fleet of bright red and blue taxi-motorbikes. They look amazingly new and smart, shining in the mid-morning sun. "Don't make the mistake of using them," says Francis, wagging his finger. "The drivers learn today –tomorrow they start!"*

. . . . . . . . . . . . .

*Now we're turning off the main drag into the outskirts of Korogocho slum. Our jeep slows down to a crawl, picking a way between wandering chickens and goats, street stalls, pavement cooking fires, and the milling crowds. There's every kind of person here, some smartly dressed and businesslike, some scrawny and poor, some bent double with age. Brown filthy water runs in a gutter along the roadside. Afro-beat and Hi-life music blares from transistors and dangling outdoor speakers hanging outside ramshackle cabins with rusty tin roofs and plaster walls painted with the logos of Coca-Cola and Sprite ("Freedom from Thirst"), where you can buy mobile phones and SIM cards, or a ticket to watch the Premier League on satellite "Slum TV". Everyone loves the Premier League here. An Arsenal scarf or a Man United flag is a precious possession.*

*"What about the Kenyan football clubs?" we ask Francis.*

*"Well, they're improving," he says, "but we prefer the Premier League."*

*We've noticed an A4 poster pinned up on lots of posts and fences in this district:*

*Clean Up The World Day*
*Korogocho & Kariobangi Slums*
*Saturday September 15th, 9am – 4pm*


*Activities include:*
*Clean Up, Sports Entertainments, Legal & Medical Surgeries*
*Participants include:*
*Residents, Lawyers, Professionals*

*I'm impressed to see local people coming together to help themselves, taking their own initiative to clean up their neighbourhood, even though everyone is struggling individually to make ends meet.*

. . . . . . . . . . . . .

*We've arrived. To our right is a colourful mural of a black John the Baptist standing in the River Jordan, with "St John's Catholic Church" in large painted letters. We pull through the gates into a neat compound behind high walls. There's a good-sized football pitch and a basketball court on one side, both with beaten-earth floors, and on the opposite side of the yard, a breeze-block school house and library, with a corrugated iron roof and brightly painted walls. There are children scampering back and forth, in grey school uniforms with red and white checked shirts, waving and smiling and giving us the thumbs-up. Beautiful eucalyptus trees grow at one end of the library, giving the courtyard a bit of shade, their pale grey and white bark and silver-green leaves really striking against the red earth.*

*We clamber out of the jeep and unfold ourselves. That has to be the most astonishing car ride I've ever taken. Lauretta introduces us to Father John, the local Catholic priest. He looks more like a sports coach, dressed in a brown tracksuit fleece and open-neck shirt, with just a small pendant cross on a leather thong. He's soft-spoken, unshaven, and tired-looking, but he has great authority and determination.*

*"Welcome. I'm very happy to see you," he says. "This is the St John's Sports Society. All around here is St John's parish. We have 300 registered members of the sports society, and 700 more occasional players, from all backgrounds. Sometimes we reach a thousand, sometimes less. We have seven teams – football, basketball, netball, karate, taekwondo – so they are used in all those teams." He points to a group standing nearby waiting to meet us. "These are some of them."*

*Now we're surrounded by this group of young men, shaking hands and introducing themselves. They're all ex-criminals who have turned their lives around. They're going to be our minders for the day.*

*"The St John's Sports Society is an oasis within Korogocho," says Father John. "We open our gates every evening and weekend to provide a safe place for children and young people to play, but above all we aim to help them develop*

*self-belief, discipline, leadership, and teamwork skills. Many of our members have gone on to become champions and represent their country in our national teams. We're trying to cultivate sports men and women as role-models, and we're setting up initiatives for people to find or create work for themselves. Self-empowerment. The slums have been created and are maintained by the politicians and the middle classes, because they know they can use them —and misuse them."*

*Korogocho grew up in the 1970s, he explains, when people began drifting from the countryside to the city in search of work. They settled, illegally, on vacant government-owned land, and now the population has grown to around 100,000 people, crammed into just one square mile of tin shacks and mud alleyways. There are few schools or health clinics, and many families share one room.*

*"The city needs the people who live in the slums," says Father John. "They do all the work – cleaners, domestic staff, professionals, public servants – but successive governments have refused to provide basic services. We have to buy clean drinking water from mobile water trucks. They drive into the slums and charge exorbitant prices for just one jerry can. Poverty and unemployment often lead to truancy, drug abuse, and crime amongst young people. Secondary school fees are expensive, and many young people drop out. Children are often playing in unsafe conditions; Korogocho is next to the city's rubbish dumps. The dumps are completely unregulated and insanitary. You can see the smoke from the burning rubbish drifting across the rooftops continuously." He points away across the slum to a dirty cloud of smoke. "The health effects of these dump sites on women and children have been documented, but still the government does nothing. They've been here for thirty years."*

*"Clean Up The World Day" is Father John's idea. He hopes it will inspire the residents of Korogocho and Kariobangi to do something positive together for their communities: clearing up rubbish, yes, but also building friendships and solidarity. The overcrowding and tension between the different Kenyan tribes, as well as the large population of Somali refugees, has created a very unstable situation here, a powder keg which often seems about to explode.*

*"We struggle, with a lot of sadness," Father John admits, "but also with hope, because God will not allow people to live like this. We believe that God also is the God of these people. The government has not invested*

*any infrastructure in the people. Our approach is building people, taking every chance to bring them back to life. Our motto is "Pamoja tunaweza" – Together, we can!"*

*It's strange to hear such fierce determination from a man who speaks so quietly. Everyone speaks very quietly here. I'm worried Barry won't catch everything, as he's a little hard of hearing.*

*Barry shares our story with the group.*

*"There is a lot of violence between young people on the streets of London. It's not unusual now for young people to be killed like our son was. We try and work for peace on the streets of London. We've come to learn how you manage here. We've come to listen. Hopefully we can absorb something that we can take back, something of the work that you do here." He introduces me and Danny: "We have nine children, so we're a big family. This is our eldest son, Danny."*

*"And the biggest," says Danny, with a big grin. Everyone laughs.*

*"Thank you for allowing us to visit you," I say. "It's important that we share, and that we take back to London the message that you give us, and we can leave our message here with you, and perhaps we can work together –for peace."*

. . . . . . . . . . . . .

*Now we're picking our way through a maze of tiny mud alleyways criss-crossed with washing lines, led by our guides. We're going to visit a family in Father John's parish who've been affected by the post-election violence. Everyone goes to great efforts to keep clean here, despite the filth everywhere. It's rare to see anyone actually dirty, or with dirty clothes. I notice lots of the huts have a bowl of water outside the front door, and then I see a man carefully washing his feet before going in. As we're clambering down the alleyways, we have to hop from one side to the other all the time because of the sewage ditches running down the middle, or put a foot either side and waddle. The gaps between houses are so narrow, there's barely room for Danny and Barry to get through. How on earth does anyone find their way here?*

*Eventually we arrive at a tiny corrugated iron hut and step inside. We have to stoop through the low, narrow doorway. The porch area looks and feels like a very small stable. Then we troop into a completely dark, very small room – three Mizens, Tom, Lauretta, and Justin, along with our photographers*

*Ken and Abby, and one of our guides from St John's. We arrange ourselves somehow in the dark, and someone strikes a match to light a kerosene lamp.*

*In the dim glow, we meet Anne, a very young mother with a tiny baby named Michael, and her sister Grace and their mother Monica. The room's surprisingly cosy. The wooden walls and earth floor are covered with plastic sacking with neatly sewn seams to make a kind of lining. We all squeeze on to wooden "bench sofas" with beautifully patterned cushions and throws, around a fine-looking wooden table – what we'd call a coffee table. There's a small TV and a radio on another table. A calendar hangs on the wall above Anne's head, entitled "The Assumption of Mary Catholic Calendar", next to a working clock and a portrait of Anne's uncle.*

*Lauretta gives them a present from CAFOD, big bags of sugar and flour. I take the baby in my arms, and ask Monica about her family. With Lauretta translating, we discover that Anne's husband Samway and her brother Bernard have both been murdered. It feels like being in a scene from a film, sitting in this tiny shack in one of the poorest places in the world, holding a tiny African baby and hearing their stories of tragedy.*

*Monica shows us a shopping bag that she's made, working in their local self-help initiative, which she can sell for 200 Kenyan shillings, about £1.25.*

*John, a friend of Samway and Bernard, comes in to tell us about what happened: mob justice. "But God sent Father John to us," he says.*

*Monica looks very sad. I wish I could stay here and do more for her. We share our story and give her a prayer card with Jimmy's picture on it. Translating, Tom says they will treasure it. I say to her, "Our sons are together in heaven."*

. . . . . . . . . . . . .

*Outside, we meet Elijah, Charles, and Patrick, young boys working at the bag-making workshop with vintage Swan sewing machines. A group of women sit around them, cutting up cement sacks to be sewn into bags. Several of them have babies on the breast. The sacks are Titanium Dioxide Anatase Rhino Cement, printed with the slogan "Building Africa". One of the boys, called Samuel, has just come out of a gang. Patrick says he was also a gangster. Another boy has no parents. One of the women says, "Most of us have lost our husbands through gang violence. Husbands are the breadwinners, so this project is helping widowed mothers to support themselves."A senior lady, who describes herself as a mother figure, says, "We have to try to keep our young people away from drugs, glue sniffing, and crime."*

*A lot of the women are commercial sex workers, so this women's collective is hoping to expand their project to get more of them away from prostitution.*

. . . . . . . . . . . . .

*Lunch is crisps, nuts, bottled water, and Coke in the St John's school hall. Coke and Sprite seem to be the order of the day here. We meet Julius and Geoffrey, who are part of the Brotherhood and Peace Initiative, which also aims to draw youngsters away from crime and prostitution by using sport and small business projects, such as making charcoal briquettes and bead-making for girls. They say they can sell a box of ten charcoal briquettes for thirty shillings. Julius and Geoffrey talk about the "tapping of talent"–singing, football, dance –saying, "Everyone has a talent."These bright young men were both on the "Most Wanted"list, Julius tells us with a grin –"Shoot to kill!"Here in the slums, he says, people don't shout, "Stop, thief!"because the thief could be shot dead running away. Tom says, "It's very good you didn't shout when that guy stole your necklace on Sunday."*

*On the rubbish dumps of Korogocho, we meet the Brothers'Self-Help Collective – a group of cheerful, rascally looking men in their twenties and thirties, who've abandoned the life of crime to create a small collective, recycling glass and metal and rearing pigs. They explain proudly that they have a democratic system of self-governance, with elected posts of chairman, vice-chairman, secretary, treasurer, and so forth, and entertain us with stories of their criminal past. The vice-chairman demonstrates his former technique for mugging –a surprise grab from behind, one arm around the neck, while the other goes for the wallet –on a fellow Brother, to everyone's amusement.*

*After hearing our story, they're full of sympathy and sorrow. I find it amazing that, in the fragility of their own existence, they have such empathy for our loss. They give us a powerful message for the young people of Britain: "Don't waste the wonderful opportunities. We would love to have the education, the provisions, the health care. Don't waste what you've been given."*

*Nearby I see a woman sifting through the rubbish with her bare hands, separating out the different types of glass. Black storks perch everywhere, pecking through the filth. The smell is unbelievable. From the summit of the rubbish dump we see a smart new Shell petrol station towering up in the heart of Kariobangi slum. There was a tragic disaster just yesterday in one of the slums: a shallow underground oil pipeline was punctured by someone driving a post down into the ground, and oil began welling up and pouring into the river. The slum-dwellers all came running excitedly with jerry cans to collect the oil, which then caught fire. The flames swept down the river and set fire to the slum, creating a huge inferno in which hundreds were killed.*

*Lauretta says the Chinese have come into Korogocho recently, marking off areas with beacons, and the Brothers are worried they may be chased off the land by the city council and the police. On the way back to our hotel, we see Chinese construction firms everywhere, working on road building, using local labour. Huge advertising signs have been erected already alongside the unbuilt roads. We ask Francis why local Kenyan firms never get a chance to tender for the work. He laughs out loud. "If you got our contractors to do it, five months later all the materials would be gone and the road surface would be full of holes."*

• • • • • • • • • • • •

*Back at our hotel, we discuss the day's visit over a beer on the terrace. "I expected it to be unbearable today, but it wasn't," I say. "It's funny, but I felt no reason to cry today. All the children I saw looked very happy."*

*"What we saw today was something to be inspired about," says Danny. "Alan Sugar would be proud – going to a dump, cutting up plastic bags, making new bags."*

*"Some of it felt familiar," says Barry, "but some not. There was a clarity of eye. You could take a trip to some of the poorest estates in the UK and you'd see a dullness in the eye, and hopelessness."*

*"I love the way the Brothers' Collective elect their chairman, vice-chairman, treasurer etc.," says Danny, with a chuckle. "Our local government could learn a lot from them."*

*Tom says, "The family we visited live in darkness. The old lady looked very distant, but gradually things thawed. When we spoke about prayer, about faith, about being one family, she took an interest. These people see white visitors relatively often, but they loved the fact that we didn't come with police or security, with guns, that we weren't afraid. One guy said, 'Change starts here,' and touched his chest."*

*I laugh suddenly. "I couldn't believe everyone has mobile phones – and they're all on Facebook!"*

*"There was a great sense of the dignity of work," says Barry.*

*"The house we went into wasn't squalid," I agree. "It was neat; there was pride and detail in the sitting room."*

*"People are each given a work tool by the St John's Sports Society," Danny tells us, "and they pay for it by doing a coaching session at the club, an hour a week, so there is dignity and responsibility."*

· · · · · · · · · · · · ·

*The next day we head into Kibera. This place has been made famous to TV audiences by Comic Relief earlier in the year, when Lenny Henry stayed here for a couple of weeks and almost couldn't take it. It was also the backdrop for the film* The Constant Gardener, *starring Ralph Fiennes and Rachel Weisz.*

*I love all the names of the shack-shops: We Define Clean, Abundant Logistics Ltd, By God's Mercy Hair Salon, One Stop Dental Clinic.*

*We arrive at the Olympic Christian Centre (Assemblies of God Christian Ministries for Physical Fitness) and meet project leader Eddie, and youth leader Kefa, an amazing young man we met last year at the Brightlights Festival in the UK. They tell us about Youth Building Bridges for Peace in Kibera (YOBBPEK), which they launched in April 2007. Violence was the norm in Kibera, they say, especially in the year of an election.*

*"What can we do, despite not being experts?" asks Eddie. "Well, we're using a participatory approach. Focusing on energetic and disenfranchised youth, we ask people,– what do you want Kibera to be? We started with forum theatre, working with Amani People's Theatre, to educate and agitate communities about issues that affect them. We've succeeded in reaching out to some of the most violent. In 2007, during the election campaigning period, there was actually a high level of tolerance amongst youth from different political affiliations, and intra-ethnic violence was minimized. The school Peace Club was not part of the original plan, but people challenged us –why don't you take it into schools? This year we're piloting an economic empowerment approach*

*as an accompaniment to peace work. Next year, 2012, is an election year. We want to reduce violence for next year."*

*Kefa says, "Kibera is known in many places, but for the wrong reasons —for what it lacks, rather than what it has to offer. Poverty leads to a lack of hope, which leads in turn to violence. The last election pushed us to our limits as peace builders. We're grateful for CAFOD's support, for someone holding our hands. We've planted a seed; now it is growing. We're expanding our networks. We're trying to build dialogue between the generations, between women and men, between youth and youth. I always say there is a pride and dignity in Kibera. There are more beggars in the city than in Kibera!"*

*I agree with this. The women I've seen in Kibera have great dignity.*

*"People in Kibera just want to be heard," Kefa continues. "Our main methodology is dialogue. Criminals who are beyond the pale get to tell their stories, to confess. We don't bring the police with us. Our approach is healing. It's wrong that people only recognize you when there's a disaster. We want people to recognize us without disaster."*

*Barry says we need to learn these lessons and take them back to the UK.*

*"You still need to ask questions and fight for justice," says Kefa. "Sometimes violence is the only language of the weak. But we're saying, let's not use that. Let's use dialogue. The existence of the slum is a sign that things are not right with the planning of the country."*

*Kibera means "forest", and it was originally a temporary camp for returning Nubian soldiers who had served the British Empire in Burma during the Second World War. This "temporary housing" solution has been here ever since.*

*Outside the offices is a little primary school yard of beaten earth and grass, with breeze-block walls brightly painted with kangaroos, elephants, giraffes, and monkeys. There are several slides and climbing frames, as well as a side yard for football. The little children, this time in bright red uniforms, cluster round us as we come out, giggling and calling, "How are you?" in chorus, over and over. Its name is the Valley of Hope Kindergarten.*

· · · · · · · · · · · ·

*Lebour Youth Group is part of YOBBPEK, a group for kids who've defected from violence and now want to do something positive. As we drive in, we see a huge black water tank, printed with the words, "Donated by Fidel Castro O. Odinga"(the son of the Prime Minister) –"God Bless Lebour." In the hall, we meet a dozen or so young men, some of whom look like quite hard nuts, with bruises, cuts, and scars. Some have a cheeky, sardonic look. This is the tough end of peace work. The atmosphere feels almost intimidating.*

*The house rules are written on the wall:*

*No smoking*
*No idling*
*No backbiting*
*No insulting*
*No ignorance*
*No any of unnecessary bad habbit*

*Several of them tell the story of the Lebour Project. It started in May 2007, trying to prepare for possible violence around the December elections. Not all of these were good guys; they were involved in "bad activities", stealing and beating people. They mobilized themselves, got a few members together, and gradually more people joined YOBBPEK. At first the focus was solely on peace, but this has branched into self-employment projects – garbage collection, car-washing, renting out their hall. All of them used to carry pistols and machetes, and were out at night doing "bad stuff", but now they've reformed. Now they run tight security around the place and don't allow crime.*

*Moses Odiero, the vice-secretary, gets up to speak. He looks like he's lived a very rough youth. His eyes are bloodshot, his face marked with scars. "We were mugging people, we were bad."I can believe it. "Now we have changed."*

*There is applause, then Barry gets up to speak. Barry explains how Jimmy was killed, how there is much gang violence in London. Lauretta translates. "We've come to learn from you. In London, people want the police to solve these problems, or the government. The message we will take back from Kibera is that change starts with individuals getting together. This is what you're doing here: initiating change yourselves, and working together."*

*Moses asks, how many years was Jimmy? On hearing he was sixteen, he says, in his deep gravelly voice, "Oh, sorry. Sorry. I feel for you."Another asks,*

*"What about the culprit?" Another asks, "Do you have any grudge in your heart?""I feel no hate," I say. "I feel sorrow for him and his family."*

*Barry says, "I have not wanted revenge, and I thank God. If I wanted revenge, it would destroy me, my relationship with my wife and my children. When we seek revenge, it's like taking a poison and expecting someone else to fall down dead."*

*I say, "Everything we do is about hope, joy, and peace."*

*"And faith," one of the boys pipes up.*

*"Yes," I say. "I had faith as a little girl, but not to the extent I do now."*

*Tom expresses the support of CAFOD in the UK, and says that he'll take a message of encouragement back, after seeing the good they're doing here in Kibera.*

*Kefa thanks us for coming. "Everyone here has a story,"he says, "usually a very sad story, but you've given us such encouragement."*

*Then there's lots of handshakes, joshing about football teams, and posing for group photographs. Moses comes up to Tom and shouts, "Give me your number! You're Catholic, I'm Catholic! I was an altar boy! I know how to do Mass! Give me your number!"*

*The murals on the wall outside show a gang of armed youths on one side – "Party A" – and on the other side, a transformed, smiling, peaceful "family of nations".*

*As we wander back through Kibera with them, we notice some decent-looking stalls, selling shoes, vegetables, fruit, hardware, and soap; we also see a magistrate's court, a mosque, butchers' shops, and slum "hotels". One of the young men, called Eddy, rides with us in the jeep and explains how politicians came into the slums after the last elections, giving out money, guns, and other weapons and encouraging people to fight their neighbours –"Go! Go and fight for your team!" The violence was shocking. People are determined not to let this happen again.*

*Every so often you see USAID or Japanese Government signs around Kibera: "This clinic was built with the help of the United States Government" and so on, but not CAFOD. Their presence is much more discreet; their support is powerful, but invisible.*

. . . . . . . . . . . . .

*We're on foot again now, weaving our way through a sea of iron roofs, TV aerials everywhere, ducking beneath the washing lines threading across all the alleyways. We're approaching the Shape The Child Foundation NGO Primary School. The school children are all dressed in clean clothes. There's Hi-life music playing in the background.*

*Genesis, the Peace Club leader, welcomes us in the school hall, with a group of children. We notice lots of other kids outside, with their faces all pressed up against the windows watching us. There are ten schools in Kibera, Genesis explains. They "shape the lives of the child" – doing drawings, making music, doing forum theatre and other peace-related activities. "They are all Peace Club members," he says, "not kids! These children are the future. They see the violence happening and sometimes they are prevented from going to school. They are affected by the violence, and we want to teach them a different way." All the children wear Peace Club T-shirts, with the slogan, "Awake & Make Peace." "We meet every Wednesday and go through our new constitution," says Genesis. "We talk about the rights of children."*

*As the children come up on stage, Mr Evans, the headmaster, tells us the school is very new, started in 2009, but over the two years, they have already seen radical change taking place. "There are lots of struggles and challenges," he says, "but to match the peace programmes taking place in Kibera, we've established the Peace Club here in the school." He introduces the fourteen-year-old pupil who's the chairwoman of the club, Tracy Akinyi, and her assistant chair. His goal, he says, is to send children out into the village as good people. Holding Jimmy's photograph, he expresses his sorrow to us, and their shared determination to work for peace.*

*Tracy introduces the song that they will sing, a Swahili song about peace. They sing strongly and beautifully, with bright voices, stepping in rhythm from side to side. Then they perform a rap poem, acting out a series of choreographed arguments, turning in chorus this way and that, and finally turning to the audience, exhorting us, "Take care –don't think I don't scare/ because if you walk without care/you'll end up nowhere!" The performance is brilliantly charismatic and funny, with great movement and dance. Genesis gets up to teach us a short clapping, clicking, and stamping routine, to see "if we are good students", and then he invites "Baba Jimmy" and "Mama Jimmy" to speak. What a lovely way to be addressed.*

*Barry pitches it very simply and very well. "Who's the most important person in bringing peace?"he asks them.*

*A pupil puts her hand up and says, "Us!"*

*"Right!" says Barry. Then I get everyone to make a fist, symbolizing anger, and then let go. I always do this in schools back home. Barry congratulates them on their work for peace, and says, "Never forget that you are special and loved, loved by God. If people tell you peace won't happen, don't believe them."*

*Kefa gets up and says, "When you sang that song, congratulations, you did so well. We are one people. No one should tell us we are different. We live in the same country, the same place. We are one. You can all be the greatest. The future belongs to you. I used to dream I would be a pilot or an engineer. I never thought I would come to live in Kibera, but I never lost hope. YOBBPEK, CAFOD, KYF —we are here for you.*

*"Some of you may have seen people who burnt their houses in the post-election. Some of you may have seen people who were raped in that time. Some of you may know people who did those things. So keep strong for peace. You want to know the future? Look at yourselves! If you keep strong, you will see forty years. Some of you are talking about AIDS. Keep strong. Keep it together and you will see forty years. It's very hard to see forty years in Kenya today. Thank you so much. You're amazing."*

*After the applause dies down, Eddy, the YOBBPEK leader, speaks: "Out of the ashes of Jimmy, something good can come." I feel so moved by these beautiful words. "I'm so grateful for this family. If you can think of this building as like an ark, a Noah's ark, then you will all be part of Noah's ark, building peace for the future."*

*Finally Tracy Akinyi gets up to give a talk that she's written herself. Her speech is so impressive, articulate, and moving, and delivered with such clarity and confidence, that afterwards Justin asks Mr Evans for a copy. Tracy's handwriting is immaculate.*

*"Distinguished guests, ladies and gentlemen, and my fellow pupils, good afternoon. I stand here bravely to give a speech about peace.*

*"Peace is the great fruit of the Holy Spirit, and peace is not involving or causing argument or violence. Some countries in East Africa are rich but still there is no peace. They are only wishing to live in peace with others and like every country around them.*

*"We can work together for the better world with men and women of goodwill, those who radiate the intrinsic goodness of humankind. Non-violence is more powerful than all the armaments in the world. Peace is mightier than the mightiest weapon of destruction devised by the ingenuity of man. Nothing good ever comes of violence. Let us be our brothers'and sisters'keepers by making peace with them even if they are our enemies.*

*"Blessed are the peacemakers, as it says in Matthew 5, for they shall be called the children of God."*

*After the applause, we ask the pupils to show us an example of their forum theatre work. Immediately, three of them jump up and act out a little sketch of an argument, with a third party intervening, sorting out the dispute, and persuading them to apologize to one another. They perform it with great gusto, but also humour, and they get lots of laughs and applause from the audience.*

*As they're filing out for their lunch break, one of the girls goes up to Justin and whispers in his ear, "I wish you write the best story!"and shakes hands, cracking a huge grin.*

*"I hope so," he says.*

. . . . . . . . . . . . .

Justin Butcher:

Not far from here on foot, we wander across a railway line into a district known as Soweto West. This is the most intimidating place so far. Our minders are constantly chivvying us to keep up and keep the group together. On one of the busy market streets, we pass Kibera's only mosque. Outside, we're introduced to a Muslim friend who happens to be going in for prayers. Only 11 per cent of Kenya's population is Muslim, and more than 80 per cent are Christians, but the faiths coexist fairly peacefully. Then, just next to a fabulously named nursery – the Flames of Hope Glory Worship Centre Day Care & Kindergarten – we come to the Soweto West Women's Peace Specific Forum: a small corrugated iron hall, with wooden benches, wooden beams, and very rough earth floor, packed with an assembly of women: some Muslim, most Christian.

Introducing the CAFOD delegation, Kefa says, with a sly grin, "During the violence, I was told it was the women telling the men to go out on the streets and fight."(Laughter and cries of "No, no!") "They said, 'If you can't wear the trousers, give them to me!'" (More laughter.) "So women are very important for peace. You want more forums. These people from CAFOD are the ones who help to fund the forums."

Eddie addresses the women in Swahili, and one of them, Sara, is introduced as the chairperson. Sara gives a brief introduction, then from the floor the most senior lady, a big feisty mama in a woolly hat with a deep voice and a dangerous-looking grin, gets up. One of the KYF volunteers translates. "Before the violence erupted," says the mama, "we knew we were electing Odinga as President. The votes were not counted on the first day, or the second day, but on the third day! We were expecting Odinga to be elected, but Kibaki was announced – and sworn in! After this, the other tribes, who were not Kikuyus, were being chased away. If Odinga was elected President, there could not be violence. The parents were called into schools, to try and encourage peace between different tribes. Now, we're trying to bring in women from different tribal groups. Previously, people were not informed. Now, they are informed and we're not expecting violence to erupt again."

She used to keep a Kikuyu person in her house. When the violence erupted, people from her own community came to punish her, because she had hidden this Kikuyu girl, taking her to another refuge elsewhere. She witnessed a neighbour looting someone's shop, someone who'd run away. When she tried to intervene, she was threatened with a machete. But she wasn't afraid, because she knew who the machete person was. Then, when the shopkeeper came back, he was killed, leaving a wife and three children.

"We are trying to bring all tribes together – Luhyas, Kambas, Luos, Kikuyus, all tribes."

Another woman tells how she saw a small child being killed in front of her. "I felt so bad. When we were taking the body to the mortuary, there were no police to help us. We're still afraid to vote, because of what happened. There are still some people living in refugee camps. The politicians live a better life than us, so we should come together and be one thing."

A Muslim woman says, "Even the police didn't maintain security. They came in and raped women and children in the same house."

Another woman says it was hard to access medical services, because even the doctors were favouring patients of their own tribe.

A beautiful young woman with large, elaborate earrings says, "The children were the most affected, because they didn't know anything. It's so hard to console the children."

Another woman describes how she was raped by people from her own tribe, because she's a little lighter skinned than most of them, so they thought she was a Kikuyu. She now has a child, but doesn't know who the father is.

"Even within households," says another, "there is domestic violence that also traumatizes the children, even in schools."

"Sometimes," says one woman, "girls are being raped by their own parents, brothers, and uncles, and this is not being reported to the police. They don't want to expose their shame to the community."

"Peace begins as a person's own responsibility," says one. "Before you can clean anyone else, you have to begin with your own actions." She tells the women not to rely on KYF and YOBBPEK for peace, but to make efforts themselves.

The older lady says, "This is a multi-tribal group which has come together for self-help economic activities, so they do a 'Merry Go Round' where they all chip in some money, and if someone's in particular need, they support them, for example with school fees. Secondary school fees are very dear."

The beautiful young lady with the earrings says, "This is a big lesson: we are the ones who suffer. Those who instigate violence are not here –they are in their comfortable houses. It's about us and it's down to us."

"Equality in society is very important."

"Through the forums, I've learned to get on with my neighbours."

The old lady explains to all the women their importance as agents of conflict management and reconciliation.

At Sara's invitation, Barry gets up to speak, but in the front row, two little boys are grinning from ear to ear and chanting, "How are you? How are you?"over and over, giggling as if the burly pink-faced shoe-mender from Lewisham is the funniest thing they've ever seen. Perhaps he is. Barry chuckles and says, "I've got some hecklers."He bends down to them. "How are you? I'm very well, thanks, how are you?"The little boys giggle, hands over their mouths, eyes and teeth shining white in the gloomy hut, and all the women laugh.

"Thank you for sharing your powerful stories," he says, straightening up. "I believe if women ran the world, it would be a safer place. How do I know this? My wife told me." (Laughter and applause.) "We're here to listen as much as speak." He tells their story, describing with particular emphasis how Tommy held Jimmy in his arms as he died. The women are rapt, their eyes glistening.

Then, as Margaret speaks, something begins to happen. Because Kefa is translating into Kiswahili sentence by sentence, Margaret has to alter her normal chatty, conversational pace of speaking and choose measured phrases, weighing each thought as it flows out. It is fascinating. These women who have poured out their stories of loss, suffering, and injustice are spellbound to hear Mama Jimmy speak at last, but because they have to wait for each phrase to be translated, what they receive first is the story of the heart – through gesture, tone, facial expression, the compassion in the eyes, the cadence in the voice. Margaret seems to grow in her presence before them, instinctively broadening not only her gesture, pace, and tone but also her vision, to reach across to them in the universal language of motherhood:

"I saw my son bleeding to death. From the start of the attack to the time that he died was three minutes. And I thank God that I was able to be there for those very last few minutes of my son's life.

"But today I am inspired – by everything that I've heard here of the work that you're doing. Although we live in different parts of the world, we're not so different. You have your children and you love your children. I have my children and I love my children. And we together are working for peace.

"We are a very ordinary family, we're not a rich family in London, and I have nine children. I have seven sons and two daughters who I love very much and, as you know, one of my sons is over there." She points to Danny.

"We were determined after the death of my son, our beautiful boy, to bring some good out of the bad thing that had happened to my son, and we wanted no more pain for any more families. So we made a decision, there and then, that we would start to work for peace. No more young people dying on the streets of London.

"Some people would say, 'Why have you come to Kenya then, if you're working on the streets of London?'But I think we can learn from each other how to bring peace. Things are not so different in London. We have many problems with young people, we have lots of gangs, and that's where the young people are killing each other, mainly with knives, sometimes with guns, although our son was killed with a glass dish.

"We go into schools and prisons and we share our son's story. We talk about how we don't have to be like this. And one of the things I heard from one of you ladies was that it starts here, in our hearts. The change must come from each and every one of us, and when we bring that change, we can take it out to each other. And that's what I'm hoping today that I'll take back, just your love, back to London.

"So I believe that we've got a strength together. I feel united with you, and when I go from here, I will take all your love with me, and I will keep you in my prayers each and every day. Because we are united, in our pain, and I'm sure there's a lot more pain that you could share with me, but you haven't, but I share the pain of many mothers in London, who I spend time with, crying because their beautiful children have been killed.

"I'm afraid that the strength has to come from us mothers. You know, I think we've seen the weakness of some men (sorry, chaps). I think the strength comes from us women. So we stand up and say,

'No more. No more young people killing each other, no more anyone killing each other, but we can do it, together.'

"We teach our children, our babies, now about the good things of life. We teach them about not taking each other's possessions, and we show them the love, and then they can grow and be the good people of this world that we need.

"I take from here the message of hope, the message of joy, and the message of peace.

"Peace will come, ladies. Peace will come, I assure you, for all your hard work and for the hard work that I know people are doing in London, so together we're united. Asante [thank you]."

"*Asante*," they murmur as one, and break into heartfelt applause. It feels like I've heard her story for the first time, in that dingy room, amongst widows and orphans and mothers of children sired by rape, women abandoned or betrayed by men, these women who have taken up their own authority to become peacemakers. I'm overwhelmed, and busy myself with notebook and tape recorder to hide my tears.

"And now," says Barry, "I shall give my wife my trousers."

"Aaah!" they exclaim delightedly, and laugh and clap again.

. . . . . . . . . . . . .

"The power of those meetings was tangible," writes Tom O'Connor. "Brothers and sisters of a single global family whose worlds had never met before were showing compassion and drawing inspiration from one another. They were privileged moments without pretension or ceremony.

"Barry and Margaret are now ambassadors for CAFOD's work. They tell the story among communities in the UK of the people they met in Kenya –people who live far away with different histories and cultures but not so different from us after all. They tell a story that resonates with all people of goodwill: if we hold together as a family and show compassion for those most in need we can find the strength to release peace even from the most tragic experiences."

. . . . . . . . . . . . .

As our jeep nudges its way slowly through the evening crowds returning from the city, returning from their jobs as cleaners, car-washers, gardeners, and security guards to spend another night in Kibera, I point out to Margaret and Barry a slogan painted on a corrugated iron fence:

"Peace Wanted Alive."

# 14

# Five Years On

Although Jimmy never lived to sit his public exams, the examination board awarded him eight GCSEs, with grades ranging from A* to C, based on his coursework and his teachers' recommendations. His headmaster at St Thomas More School, Markus Ryan, described it as a "fantastic achievement for a boy who didn't find academic work easy". His Religious Education coursework, which earned him an A, contains two notable answers, in his slightly hesitant handwriting:

"Jesus told us, 'Thou shalt not murder', but people still do it."

"The Parable of the Good Samaritan answers the question, 'Who is my neighbour?' Everyone is your neighbour. You don't need to like them, just respect them."

During his sermon at the Hyde Park Vigil in September 2010, at which Jimmy's story and presence were felt so powerfully, Pope Benedict quoted these words from the writings of Cardinal Newman:

"God has created me to do Him some definite service; He has committed some work to me which He has not committed to another. I have my mission – I never may know it in this life, but I shall be told it in the next."

If these lines could serve as Jimmy's epitaph, then the thoughts with which Newman completes this reflection in his *Meditations on Christian Doctrine*, equally might be taken to describe his parents' calling:

"Somehow I am necessary for His purposes, as necessary in my place as an Archangel in his – if, indeed, I fail, He can raise another, as He could make the stones children of Abraham. Yet I have a part in this great work; I am a link in a chain, a bond of connection between persons. He has not created me for naught. I shall do good, I shall do

His work; I shall be an angel of peace, a preacher of truth in my own place, while not intending it, if I do but keep His commandments and serve Him in my calling."

Or, as Barry himself puts it, "We are very conscious that this is our life's work. I won't use the term career, but this seems to be our life's work. It would seem more drawn towards the prison visits than anything else. We've always said we want something good to come out of Jimmy's death, and it already has. Even if we do nothing else now, there's been the Jimmybuses, the prison visits, the work in schools, the hundreds of interviews, the work with Citizens UK, the founding of the City Safe Havens, our work with police chiefs and politicians, our speaking engagements, the Caféof Good Hope, this book…It's almost like God is saying, 'I have given you a learning, a learning which is denied most people. Use it. Use it.'"

During the trial, Margaret expressed her conviction that "Jimmy was going to die at that moment. We had no say in it."This marks an important step in her understanding of the meaning or purpose of Jimmy's life, defined by the fact and nature of his death. In an interview recorded shortly after our visit to HMP Huntercombe in January 2011, I asked her whether she believed that Jimmy's death was somehow part of God's plan.

"Undoubtedly," she replies. "I think God has a plan for all of us – but Jimmy's life was mapped out from the moment he was conceived. We've talked about Jimmy being different anyway, but there was a set plan for Jimmy. Some would say, 'but he was taken so violently…' and yes, he was, and yes, he was fearful, but it was all part of the build-up for most of what we're doing. If Jimmy's life was meant to be sixteen years and one day, it was a very precious life and a well-lived, well-loved life. When you do not have any regrets because you know he's had a good life, and if God was ready to take him, then you can kind of live with that. I pray, and I think, every day, that if Jimmy was taken to help the young people of this country, of this world, then I can live with that.

"Barry doesn't take exactly the same line as me on this, but he does say that, after Jimmy's death, he had such a strong sense of calling that he wonders whether maybe this was meant to be. That raised a few eyebrows. As he says, much fruit has been borne out of this. You know, some people bear fruit within this life, some after this life."

I say, "Some people, hearing that, or reading this book, will be bound to ask, 'But how can you believe that the untimely death of your son, full of youth and potential, with everything to live for, and through such a violent act, which has resulted in such damage to the life of your family – how can you believe that these things were planned by God?'"

Margaret replies, "I can only say that I haven't actually got the answer to that. But I still feel that it was planned, that Jimmy wouldn't live more than sixteen years and one day. I don't think God ultimately gives us pain, in the way that we've suffered, but I think what happens, when you have this pain, is that He's there to help you and guide you through that difficult time.

"I'm not saying that God planned Jimmy's death in the way it was, but by Jimmy's death being in the way it was, maybe it will help other young people not to suffer the way that Jimmy did. Because we know that Jimmy's safe. We know that he's in heaven. We will seehim again. I haveno doubt about that. But I don't think I've got the answers; I just know, I just do know that… He's almost told me, in fact He has, in my prayer time, it's come very clearly: Jimmy is safe, Margaret. You don't have to worry about him. He's safe.

"I don't believe I'm particularly articulate or very academic. I have a simple faith. I believe that God loves me and I love Him. I don't know what else I need to know."

"We look at everything about death," says Barry, "the timing of death – it's going to come to us all. Some lives are long; some are not. There is eternal life, we believe. There is an eternity. We're promised Paradise. We don't know. I say openly, I've no idea what there is, but I believe there is something –and it's a question of where you enter this something. Jimmy's in Paradise now. Jimmy's happy. Jimmy's safe. Where do we join it along the line? Where do we join the people who've died before us, some very young? Is it more tragic that someone dies at a day old or a hundred years old? I don't know.

But this is all part of a process, a continuum…we're all going to die. A baby born yesterday is going to die one day. But we tend to push this thought to one side and behave as if we were going to live for ever. Not in this world."

"As Catholics," says Margaret, "we tend to pray to the saints a lot. But we also pray to Jimmy –to intercede to God on behalf of all the young people, that they will live fulfilled lives, that our streets will be safe, and we're asking Jimmy, almost, to take care of the young people. Now, we didn't know whether we were doing the right thing by doing that, so we went and spoke to an elderly priest, who's full of wisdom, whom we could trust. If he'd said to us, 'No, you absolutely can't do that', then we wouldn't, but he said, 'Of course you can.' For me, Jimmy is our saint in heaven. He was a wonderful, loving boy, full of good nature, kindness, and generosity, and I hope and pray, through Jimmy interceding to God, that there will be a change. Some would say, times are no better –but I do believe people are thinking more now. I'm not saying it's just through Jimmy. I'm not. But I do think that Jimmy's death almost…well, Cliff Lyons summed it up when he said, 'Jimmy's death woke up middle England', and we had to start asking, 'How can someone go out at eleven-thirty in the morning, into a baker's shop, and be killed?'"

"I've been reading recently about 'the sanctity of the everyday'," says Barry. "When Margaret's talking about this goodness that's coming from Jimmy's death, you get a sense of this thirst – that everybody wants this peace; you do feel there is a thirst out there. Even guys in prison have still got that thirst, that thirst for something better, something good, decent, pure… Is that their quest? Do we get sucked into behaving the way we do? Did Jake get sucked down some sewer to behave the way he did? And how do we get ourselves back? As Margaret said, 'Everybody deserves to be forgiven, including the killer of my son.'"

Against the backdrop of this discussion, it seems bitterly ironic to reflect that Jake Fahri, who has pursued a path of violent aggression for most of his life, should survive two near-fatal stabbings by a hair's breadth since he's been in prison, while the peaceable Jimmy, who refused to fight him, sustained such horrific injuries at his hands that he bled to death in a matter of minutes. If one seeks to find meaning and purpose in Jimmy's untimely death, one cannot avoid the flipside of such questions: for what purpose has Jake Fahri been "preserved"?

Pondering Jake's fate, Barry says, "You'd hate to think that a violent person goes into prison, and an even more violent person comes out. You would like to think there would be some sort of change. People have said, 'Well, what if this person asks for forgiveness?' It's not our forgiveness this person needs; it's God's forgiveness. We believe we're all made in the image of God – from the Old Testament, from Jeremiah, 'Before I formed you in the womb, I knew you.' To destroy the image of God? That's where the forgiveness needs to come. And if this person genuinely seeks God's forgiveness (and only the person and God will know if that's genuine), then who are we to say no?"

Margaret says, "I believe that many people in prison have not had the love of a mother, and maybe I want to give them some love, so that they might feel people do actually care about them, then maybe they'll come out changed, rather than commit the crime again. So it's about caring in our society. It's about change. I've taken people who've committed murder in my arms and you can feel their pain, and I just feel that's where I'm being called. It's not because I'm this 'good Christian lady'. I'm just a mother. God gave me the role of a mother. Our Lady is the image of motherhood, not just the joyful side of motherhood, but also suffering motherhood. Just knowing that Mary's there, when I need the comfort of a mother. I didn't have a mum after Jimmy was killed. But I had Mary the Mother, and that was probably where I got my strength to go on. Because Barry and I would pray all the time, and most of our prayers were the Our Father and three Hail Marys, and they would get us through the deepest, darkest moments in the middle of the night. Those first few days were really awful, and we wouldn't have got through it without our prayers.

"I always wanted to go to Lourdes, and I went just a month before Jimmy was killed. It's the most amazing place. I don't mean all the shops selling souvenirs –they don't mean very much to me –I mean the real presence of Our Lady there. She suffered so much. She saw her Son, nailed to a cross, and Simon said to her, 'A sword will pierce your heart as well', and it did. I feel I've been a mother to many people in life, not just to my children, and that is a call to care, but it's also a call to suffer. I think I've probably had more than my fair share of suffering, but if that's God will for me, then I will follow His way. I couldn't live any other life than I lead.

"This journey –I just think each day you realize how important God is in your life and how – how do people manage without Him? You can hear just in my story, there have been difficult times, and I know that it was God who helped me through it. I knew that He was there for me, and I wouldn't have got through it any other way.

"We find ourselves going into some extraordinary situations, but we just go home each night, cook the dinner, look after Samantha and George, do the washing-up, and fall asleep in front of the telly! We're very ordinary!"

"We don't want to come across as some kind of righteous 'God squad'," says Barry. "We just believe, when we're in these situations, that this is of God."

. . . . . . . . . . . . .

As Margaret and Barry embrace their public role as advocates or ambassadors for peace with ever-greater confidence and authority, there is a sense that their children are beginning to emerge from a "limbo period"that has shrouded the family ever since Jimmy's death. Danny and his girlfriend Fay now have a baby daughter, Eva, and live above the shoe-mender's shop, which Danny runs. Tommy has embarked at last on his long-postponed travels to the Far East. Billy has taken a leading role in the management of the Jimmy Mizen Foundation, while Bobby manages the Caféof Good Hope, with Joanne working shifts here and there.

After three years of sleeping on the floor of his parents' bedroom, George has moved finally into his own room. He's now a keen member of the Jimmy Mizen Foundation fundraising group. Harry's moved on to a new job and each year, he and James organize the "Sparkle

Football Cup" in Jimmy's memory. Joanne has done fundraising climbs of Ben Nevis and Snowdon. "I've enjoyed doing the climbs and the fundraising work in Jimmy's memory," she says, "but how I wish he was still here. I think of Jimmy and what happened to him all the time, but I listen to my mum's faith and I know he's safe. But if only we could turn back the clock."

Samantha's life has become narrower since Jimmy's death, Margaret says. "Her dependence on routine has become greater than ever. She no longer wants to go on holidays, or to social events, and it's hard to get a smile out of her."

Money is a constant struggle for all the family, and most of the children still live at home. "I'm sure they'll get fed up with living at home eventually," Margaret continues, "but I have to say, the financial effect it can have on a family is not something most people are aware of. If you see in the paper that some young lad has been killed, most people don't think of the consequences – how, beyond the grief and the tragedy and so on, it affects the family's finances."

"You almost feel like you've lost ten years," says Billy. "Leaving aside the year after Jimmy's death, I'd done a four-year apprenticeship in catering, then four years at university, and then Jimmy died two weeks after I'd finished my degree. Not that I'm whining in any sense, but you get knocked back professionally as well as personally; you almost feel you have to start the whole journey again. And we've made a commitment to carry on Jimmy's memory and legacy, and that became more important than gaining a personal career, and it still is, but it's really tough – trying to rebuild your whole life, as well as dealing with all the emotional issues. Two days before Jimmy died, I was sitting outside a Pizza Express with a friend of mine, a bottle of wine, the sun was shining, and I said, 'Life doesn't get much better than this.' And then two days later it all changes. I regret saying that now."

When Tommy described his struggle with depression, trauma, and "survivor's guilt" to me, he talked a lot about his weight. "I've put on three stone since Jimmy died," he said. "I should lose weight really, get fit, start running again, but part of me's afraid to. You know, part of me wants to stay overweight, because if I lost a lot of weight and got fit and got faster, that would somehow prove that if I'd been fitter back then, I could have run faster when Jimmy needed me at the bakery and maybe I would have got there in time to save him. And that would mean I'm to blame, for not being fit enough to rescue my little brother."

"Jimmy was my connection with staying young," says Danny. "All the family used to go down to the coast at Christmas time, to the same hotel. That last Christmas, I'd just come back from travelling and turned up out of the blue, and that night, we all ended up going out to a nightclub – me, Billy, James, Harry, Tommy, Joanne, and Jimmy. Jimmy was only fifteen, but we all got in, spent the evening there, had a few beers. Jimmy and Harry were up on the stage, having a laugh – it was just a really good memory, not just of Jimmy wanting to be with us, but also of us still wanting to be young, just enjoying each other's company, just unbothered young people who never really let things get on top of us. It's not until a few years later you begin to look back and realize that things have changed; we've lost a little of that happy-go-lucky time together. Things are a bit more tense.

"All I can remember after Jimmy died was feeling, 'You've got to focus, got to get the shop open, make sure everyone has money, especially Mum and Dad.' He died on the Saturday and I think the shop was open on the Tuesday or Wednesday afterwards. I almost despise myself for going back so early, but at the same time all I could think about was that we needed money to pay the bills so Mum and Dad didn't have to worry about it at all. In private as well as in public as a family I think we've been really strong. I'm not saying we've been happy all the time, but we have been strong."

When I ask the brothers about Margaret's sense of a pre-ordained plan for Jimmy's life, there is an uneasy chuckle.

"My parents have a very strong faith," says Billy, "and I have to be careful about what I say, as I don't necessarily share their views. If someone asks me, did God help me, I tend to answer, well, He helped my parents. They believe, and through their faith, it has helped us. One of the things which wound me up at the time was this thing of trying to find an answer, and God being the answer to those questions of 'Why?' Why did this happen? I accept that, through Mum and Dad, their belief has helped us – their strength which they then pass on to us."

"When I was younger I was interested in religion," says Bobby. "As I've got older it's not necessarily been a massive part of my life, apart from through my parents. Did God intend it? Well… I feel, it has happened, and you adapt, and God has helped them and through their strength helped us, which is great."

"What helps me is being together in our family," says Danny. "It's probably the one thing I do disagree with my mum about – this idea that God had a plan, that this was Jimmy's plan. I can't believe that myself; maybe I don't want to believe that. Being part of a church community helps, coming together to talk about things, share things. One of the interesting things I've noticed is the amount of people who've been non-believers, or of different religions, who've come to Mum and Dad, maybe in the shop, maybe somewhere else, and said, 'Will you pray for me?'"

He continues, "For me there's no tension at all between our lives and Mum and Dad's work in prisons, work for the Foundation. I think Mum and Dad were born to do this. Their life has always been about us, their children, what we're doing, and they've supported us all the time. Let's forget about Jimmy for a second. Mum was the youngest in her family, little Marny-Potts, treated as the youngest, then she had a baby at nineteen, not married, which was really frowned upon for that generation, then met Dad and they had me, Bill, Tommy, Bob, Samantha with the Down's syndrome – a lot of people fall apart, but it seemed to make Mum and Dad stronger. Also, with my sister Jo having a baby when she was a teenager, even younger than Mum, and she's had mental health issues, and Mum and Dad didn't shy away from this –they've embraced it and helped as much as they can. Everything they've done –they've worked harder and harder and harder for all of us, and now they've found their voices and they're getting out there and doing what they were born to do.

"When Dad first took over the business because his dad had died, he was young and he had to support his family. Then, when he got married, he was working six and a half days a week to look after us all, then he bought another shop and he was working seven days a week, so all his life has been focused on helping us. So now we're doing something which is helping him and Jimmy. My parents are always truthful. I know Mum sometimes wonders whether what she said immediately after the tragedy was right, but it was her true feelings. It was how she felt, not trying to be clever or anything like that, but just what was inside here, here" – he touches his chest –"how she loves Jimmy and how she feels for the Fahri parents. It was her honesty coming out. I think the work my parents are doing is absolutely amazing."

After a pause, he says, "I can't believe it's been four years since he died. For me, it seems as fresh as yesterday."

"One thing I've found hard," says Bobby, "is trying to remember Jimmy's voice. He used to kind of grunt and say, 'Aw'ight?' when he came home from school, and now I really struggle to remember how he spoke. And as the years go on, you think, I don't want to completely forget how he sounded. That's such an important thing; it's the way I remembered him, you know, with a deep voice and a kind of Cockney accent. That's quite tough."

"The other day I was sitting in the Foundation office," says Billy, "and it's just weird to think that, in that four years, we've built the coffee shop and the office and got the Jimmybuses off the ground – tangible things, and they wouldn't be there if Jimmy hadn't died. The office and coffee shop would probably be an African bar or something – that's what everyone seems to want to do in Hither Green! – or maybe still a car spares shop as it was before. It's weird to sit down and reflect, the reason these things are there and helping the community (and they do) is because Jimmy died. I've no idea where we would be individually, if he hadn't. It's just weird. And on the one hand, I wish the coffee shop wasn't there and I wish Jimmy hadn't died, but you've kind of got to face reality, which is a horrible thing sometimes, but I kind of say to myself, you can either dwell on the sadness or try and do something positive.

"People talk about 'closure'. I've no particular need for 'closure'and I don't even seek it. I'd hate to have 'closure'; I almost feel it's closing off Jim, which is the last thing I'd do. I don't need statistics to prove it, but some good has definitely come, and good will continue to come from our loss. Maybe in five years'time, some kid will come up to us and say, 'It was the Jimmy Mizen Foundation that helped me along my way'–you know, that we had a part to play."

"I like to think that we can be proud as well of Jimmy's achievements," says Danny. "Because of the type of person he was, you know, the Foundation lives around what he did as a person, and we're not trying to look at what happened to him – we're looking at what he was as a person, a lad that wanted to work, wanted to earn money, that was generous, wanted to be with his family, that would help strangers at times, help friends… so, in some ways, you're proud of what he's achieved himself – while not being here himself. It's all in his name. It's all part of Jim's legacy, what he's left behind, just an average sixteen-year-old boy, but he can show people of his age what you can achieve.

"One day Billy gave a bollocking to one of the lads who work in the café. He's about seventeen, good lad, but he came in one day and he'd obviously been drinking the night before, so Billy took him out the back to the garden for a word. They always know they're in trouble if Billy takes them in the garden! And he says, 'Listen, if you come in here, wearing the T-shirt, working in the café, representing the Foundation, and you're behaving like this, it actually disrespects my brother. It's in Jimmy's memory. You working here is a part of his legacy. We expect you to respect that, respect the type of lad he was, by coming in with a professional attitude.'"

"You have a responsibility, if you're training young people," says Billy. "And to the young boy's credit, OK, he was sent home, but he left thinking about what he'd done, came back a couple of days later to apologize, and he's changed."

"It can be a pressure," says Bobby, "if you're working in the café. You don't want to have an off-day, because if a member of the public sees you not at your best, it can reflect badly on the Foundation."

"And because the Foundation is so well known," says Billy, "it's kind of like everything we do has a bearing. That's why we like each other's company so much, because if you want to be yourself it doesn't go any further. It's a time when we can relax and be, without the pressure to be on your best behaviour. But that comes, I suppose, with any organization that's well established in the media."

. . . . . . . . . . . . .

The media interest in Barry and Margaret and the work of the Foundation has continued unabated and is not focused solely on the nature of Jimmy's death. Just as Danny says, the Jimmy Mizen Foundation has become known as an organization that celebrates and upholds the energy and potential of youth, affirming the essential decency and merit of the majority of young people. And Margaret and Barry, despite – or perhaps because of – their genuine humility, have become known as influential public figures in their own right. They are no longer "just" the parents of Jimmy Mizen, whatever they may say or think.

In an almost hyperbolic article for *The Daily Telegraph* written just before Christmas 2011, Mary Riddell cites the Mizens as transformative, defining figures in the battleground which she calls the "politics of the soul":

> Although his campaign has made him a household name, Jimmy's father Barry is a modest man. Last week, I chaired a debate in which he told the audience: "I'm not a public speaker or a teacher. I'm just a dad. What happened is incredibly sad, but so are all murders. So do not feel sorry for me. Do not think I will make you cry. Mine is a message of hope."
>
> Barry Mizen's message, that retribution will not end violent crime, is reiterated in his essay for a Fabian pamphlet offering ideas for Labour's criminal justice review. Mr Mizen is no political tribalist, and in an age when leaders genuflect to calls for retributive justice, no party fully embraces his creed. That is their loss, and ours...

Neighbourhoods are changed and eras defined by people like Barry Mizen. As the year of the protester and the rioter nears its end, the economic crisis has demonstrated the frailty of the once omnipotent. Influence has leached away from power blocs, such as the US and the EU, and from tinpot tyrants and democratically elected leaders alike.

Much of that power vacuum will be filled, for good or ill, by citizens. As the economic crisis deepens, and solutions become more elusive, the politics of the spreadsheet will give way to the politics of the soul...

Folklore decrees that adversity produces civic heroism. The Blitz spirit may owe more to myth than to reality, but its obverse − hatred and unrest − demand great leaders able to switch the mood from ugly to benign. It is a mark of widespread political failure that the heirs of Churchill and FDR are thus far to be found in enclaves far from Westminster.

One such centre is the Caféof Good Hope, in south-east London, where residents drink coffee and eat cupcakes in soft chairs under posters that recall the brief life of Jimmy Mizen. Next door, the foundation set up in his name is manned by his brothers, distinguishable by the feathers tattooed on their wrists as a symbol of forgiveness.

On a public stage last week, Barry Mizen said that he wanted cross-party consensus on countering violence and unrest. He emailed me later to repeat that wish. In his essay, he spelled out the legacy he dreams of for his son. "Not one of anger, vengeance or fear, but one of hope and peace."As the parliamentary year closes today, all political leaders should offer their amen.

Echoing these thoughts in a piece for *The Independent*'s website published just before the local government elections across the UK in May 2012, the iEditor Stefano Hatfield writes:

Barry Mizen is an extraordinary man.

He has risen above the most life-changing, sorrowful and nonsensical event that most parents could imagine: the death of a child through an act of violence. He is unwavering in his attempt to turn the May 2008 murder of his son Jimmy into a force for good...

If I cannot imagine the pain his family endured, I can scarcely comprehend their courage.

They set up the Jimmy Mizen Foundation to "promote the good in young people"and opened the Caféof Good Hope next door. Yesterday, Barry was on the radio. He was promoting "safe havens"for young people in places like shopping centres, where they can shelter if they feel threatened. Barry was adamant: that locking up knife carriers isn't the answer, education is.

This was the day after news that, despite David Cameron's election manifesto soundbite that he would lock up all knife carriers, it only happens in one in five cases. Cue outrage. But not from Barry and Margaret Mizen, who tour Britain raising awareness of the consequences of knife crime.

Barry argues that when his son was born in 1992, the prison population was half what it was when he died. Locking up our disaffected young will never solve the problem. Instead the Mizens campaign, fund-raise and actually make a difference.

You will learn a lot more at jimmymizen.org than you ever will from an election pledge.

. . . . . . . . . . . . .

"We've tried to keep our feet on the ground," says Margaret. "Yes, we have been privileged to do a lot of things. I mean, our lives have changed, completely. But the most important thing is, we are very ordinary people. That has not changed; we may have done something pretty 'national stage', but I go home because I've got dinner to cook. George comes home from school and Sam from her day centre, and I come home and make sure there is dinner on the table. We are just so ordinary. We say we have had a cup of tea with Prince Charles, yes, but we then go home to our ordinary lives. I don't get carried away with the celebrity of it all. Many things have changed in my life since Jimmy's death, many things that used to be important are less so now, and many things have taken on a new meaning. Prior to losing Jimmy, if I had come anywhere near someone famous I would have been completely star-struck, but not now. Now, I can also see the person behind the celebrity, and they have the same hopes, fears, and anxieties as the rest of us. When it comes down to it, we are all just people. All any of us really need is to be wanted, valued, and loved; all we really need to know is, Do I matter? Am I of value? Do you love me? And it's the answers we get to those questions that determine the people we become.

"If someone said to me today, 'What would you like?' – well, I'd like to go back to 2008 and how life was. We were pretty busy people, and Barry and I had our little holidays together, just because we were so busy with all the things we were involved in, we got tired sometimes… but take me back to then and just being a mum. Just a mum – that's what I want to be. It is great, going to speak in all sorts of places, but all I really want to be is a mum. I feel as though it was taken away from me a little bit, by what happened to Jimmy. I feel as though part of my life was taken away from me. I am no longer just a mum. Does that make sense?

"Sometimes I wake up and I've got this big weight on my shoulders. It lays heavy, and I'm trying to straighten up. I want my arms round him so I can cuddle him and comfort him and keep him warm and I can't do that."

"People talk a lot about closure after a death," says Barry. "I think it's because they want everything to be all right again, for you to 'get over' it, so they can feel better. I don't want closure as, in a way, it will be like shutting something out of my life. What happened is part of who I now am, and I learn to live with that. When someone is ripped out of the heart of a family in the way Jimmy was, it redefines you as a person. I am now a different person to the one I was.

"The pain that can come on because of what happened, the sheer innocence of what happened, it hurts. It starts in the pit of your stomach and just wells up, like being folded in half and squashed in a vice; it hurts so much that I double over. But it comes less and less frequently now, which worries me —am I losing my contact with Jimmy? I welcome this pain when it comes, because it somehow connects me to my boy.

"When Jimmy's body was in the mortuary, before he was buried, I used to drive down there at night and sit in the car park. It was a way of being near to him. There are times when I still feel him around me in the house, when he still is close. And others when I don't. The sofa in the sitting room, the last place he sat before he went out that Saturday morning, had to go. Margaret couldn't bear it being there. Of course we have many pictures of him around the house and many of his belongings...

"You miss him terribly. But at the same time, there's a little bit of joy. There's a calmness. We can't explain what happens after death. We don't know. But what we firmly believe is that this life is not all there is. We believe there is something other."

"I know I'll see Jimmy again," says Margaret. "I don't sit here and say, 'Perhaps I will.' I don't doubt it. I know I'll see Jimmy again. And that keeps me going."

. . . . . . . . . . . . .

Jimmy's grave in Hither Green Cemetery is like a woodland shrine, shaded by surrounding sycamore trees, strewn with flowers, gifts, votive candles, and wooden crucifixes knotted around with the school ties of friends who are no longer schoolchildren. Leaning against a tree next to the grave is Jimmy's old guitar, slowly disintegrating as the weather and seasons take their toll over the years since his sixteenth birthday. His old school friends will be celebrating their twenty-first birthdays soon, graduating from university, travelling the world, starting careers, getting married, setting off on their journeys into adult life, but not Jimmy. His brothers and sisters will grow up and grow older, and have children of their own who will never know Jimmy in life. The decaying artefacts here at his grave speak with heartbreaking poignancy of his absence, but also of a bitter-sweet paradox: that as his physical presence dwindles from the earth and the physical reality of his life recedes into memory, so all that is best, truest, and brightest about Jimmy —his sparkling spirit, eternally young — is set free, soaring up from the dust of mourning to inspire and transform lives in the world which he has left behind.

A few months before Jimmy died, two girls in his year at school were killed in a road traffic accident. The funerals were attended by all the pupils, and afterwards they talked to each other about their own mortality and what they would like people to say about them after they died. After Jimmy's death, some of his friends told Margaret and Barry about this conversation. Apparently Jimmy had said: "I just want to be remembered."

He is.

The
**Jimmy Mizen**
Foundation

Patron: Archbishop Vincent Nichols

Thank you for reading this book about our Jimmy.

I want you to take hope and encouragement from all that we do.

Please don't feel sorry for us but take Strength and determination to work for Change. It starts with each one of us. lets work together to bring Peace in memory of our fine young People who have lost their lives to Violent crime

all my love
Margaret 'X'

Charity number: 1130228 | 214 Hither Green Lane, London, SE13 6RT | 020 8852 7855 | info@jimmymizen.org | www.jimmymizen.org